I0478379

DESERVE to LEAD

Leadership Hacks from the Front Line

RICHARD BROWN

RICHARD BROWN

DEDICATION

This book is dedicated to that motivated soul whose intention is to apply their strengths, talents and perspective to helping to make an organization, any organization, more efficient through effective and inspirational leadership. At the same time, they are committed to developing those on their team to become leaders themselves. That person who is genuinely interested in knowing the members of their team they serve well beyond their job description and their performance review. They want to know their team as people, with lives, challenges, victories, and fears, not as employee identification numbers under their supervision.

The individual this book is dedicated to is not famous...yet. Will they ever be? Perhaps. But one thing I can assure you is that someday, possibly twenty to thirty years from now, the individual this book is dedicated to will be the answer to "the question." When one of their teammates from the past is sweating through an important interview, or socializing with colleagues at a corporate cocktail party, and someone asks them, "Who was the person that was the most inspirational leader you ever had the pleasure to work with?" The answer will be the individual to whom this book is dedicated.

It is my passionate hope that the answer to that question will be YOU! Perhaps that will be because you took the interviews in this book to heart. You were able to glean some degree of insight into the responsibilities and rewards of leadership from the individuals featured here. Afterwards, you sought out the remaining interlocking pieces of the puzzle to form your own image that made you an individual that **"DESERVEs To LEAD."**

TABLE OF CONTENTS

RICHARD BROWN

The spectacular yet forbidding summits of the Grand Teton range beckon just beyond the snow tipped buds of the aspen trees. The ominous, silent movement beyond the branches tells me that I should focus on my task at hand, and move along briskly. Brushing the freshly fallen snow from my gear, I catch the occasional glimpse of my unknown neighbors in the distance. Their presence was subtle throughout the night, but as a chilly dawn breaks, their intentions become obvious. It is my goal to get to a place where my singular presence is not such an overwhelming disadvantage for me. Securing the bed roll to the back of my saddle is my final task, and as I accomplish it, I am startled by the sudden appearance of nearly one hundred members of the local tribes, along with their comrades in arms from other territories, descending upon me from above. Choosing a condo on the tram line transporting skiers from the base area to the top may not have been the best of options after all.

While the setting I am in may be ideal, I am afraid I am going to have to delay writing the remainder of my great western novel for another time. The scenery may be spectacular, but a more significant event is taking place in the shadow of the Teton Tramway.

As I write this, I am on a weekend getaway with an old friend from my corporate days, and two other friends of his. Their mission is to ski as many vertical feet as possible during a weeklong stay in Jackson Hole, Wyoming. My own mission is to simply carve some turns on a new mountain, create another life experience and catch up with an old friend.

No one is here to discuss politics, last night's Academy Awards, or to plan future strategy for our respective organizations. Oddly enough however, a phenomenon continues to take place during our stay that I can only hope to do justice to in this introduction. I am on a ski trip with peers, and leadership is breaking out everywhere!

Forty-eight hours into the weekend, with no real significant mission to rely upon, every member of this herd has displayed their own propensity as leaders. Whether it be assuming command of the task of acquiring and managing last night's pizza delivery, planning and executing the menu for traditional egg and sausage sandwiches this morning, or gathering and transporting the beer bottles to the hot tub last night—WITHOUT—violating the house rules of "no glassware in the pool area," all of us have seized upon an opportunity to lead at various times during our stay.

Four "old guys." A simple boy's ski weekend. Every one of them accomplished in their careers. With only skiing a maximum amount of vertical feet identified as a measurable goal, they cannot help but exercise leadership. It is a beautiful thing to behold!

If you attend one of my seminars, classes, workshops or training sessions, you will hear me enthusiastically express a principle very early on:

QUESTION: "What is a group of people with no task to accomplish called?

ANSWER: "Happy hour."

That theory was aptly demonstrated during our time at the Teton Club. Happy hours were certainly in effect, but just as obvious was the exercise of leadership as demonstrated in the examples above. As soon as a mission was identified, leadership sprouted. Not at the command of anyone, but simply because it was the right thing to do.

This book is a documentation of leadership behaviors and philosophies demonstrated by individuals in the same "herd" as the folks as my ski buddies. While all were significantly accomplished in their own rights—neither my ski buddies, nor those featured in this book—are folks you most likely have ever heard of, with one notable exception. They are successful, but they are certainly not famous, and

THAT IS THE MAIN REASON THAT YOU SHOULD READ THIS BOOK!

The bookshelves in my office are no different than those of anyone who has a desire to enhance their leadership abilities. John C. Maxwell, Gen. Norman Schwarzkopf, Joe Torre, John

Wooden, Sheryl Sandberg, Warren Bennis and many more line my shelves. All names that are more than familiar to my fellow "leadership geeks." Certainly, there is a wealth of perspective that you can acquire by studying those leaders. But this does not provide you with everything a budding leader requires. This book attempts to help plug those gaps.

Diminishing someone's value in the field of leadership development because they are famous would not only be wrong, it would be silly and that is not my intention. A primary reason one is successful at leadership is because of behaviors they have adopted and consistently displayed. But let's be honest. Stature, position, experience and stars on a collar have a certain amount of impact as well. Before a word is even uttered, or an example ever set by that esteemed individual, a certain amount of respect and obedience is generated simply through reputation. If you have obtained that level of street cred, more power to you!

All leaders must start somewhere. That is what this book is about, servant leadership without fame. For nearly half a century, I have had the distinct privilege, honor and good fortune to work with incredible leaders. Truth be told, there have also been a few clueless leaders interspersed in that experience as well. It is important that I point out that none of the "clueless" examples are included in this discussion. Interestingly, I learned as much from the clueless leaders as I did from the others.

The leaders interviewed in this book are not famous…yet. They are very effective. Every day, these individuals get it done. No magic, no fame, simply the sincere and consistent execution of the basic tenets of leadership.

My previous book, *"Become THE LEADER Your PEOPLE DESERVE"* outlines the philosophies of leadership I believe are the core values necessary to any effective and inspirational leader in detail. The purpose of this effort is to document the success in leadership one can achieve by adopting those core values.

I have known each of the individuals featured in these interviews for some time. I have worked with each of them in some manner over the course of my leadership experience and I am blessed to call them my friends. Their contributions here are in no way the result of random choice. I asked them to allow me to interview them because they have lived a lifestyle reflecting the core values of a leader.

I hope that you read each interview from the perspective that these folks are just like you. Whether you are beginning your tenure as a leader, possess your own wealth of experience leading, or simply desire to make an impact of significance on those you encounter, the discussions that follow should provide significant food for thought. Just remember, these folks are **just like you**. They are effective, as well as inspirational, because of the behaviors they have adopted in serving those they lead.

So, grab a beverage, pull up a chair, and join my friends and me as we have a "jam session" regarding what it takes to "DE**SERVE** to LEAD."

RICHARD BROWN

MY LEADERSHIP VISION

If you are on a quest to find the single and solitary book that will be a standalone reference to make you an effective and inspirational leader, I am sorry to inform you that this is not going to be it.

My previous book: *"Become THE LEADER That Your PEOPLE DESERVE,"* was a detailed discussion about my experience with regards to leadership. I covered the fundamentals and foundations I consider critical in the process, as well as several examples of tactics that are useful in exemplifying the core values of any effective as well as inspirational leader.

A caveat that was expressed early on was the need to understand John Maxwell's Law of Process. An image of what it takes to be a memorable leader is not completed overnight. Like a puzzle, it is a collection of many different experiences and events that allow you to develop leadership skills. But you do not start a puzzle with a random middle piece. Imagine that my books are me standing at the card table with you, helping you find the critical four corner pieces to allow you to begin construction of your image. Just for good measure, I'm also going to give you a piece for the center of your puzzle through the interviews in this book.

Not a puzzle sort of person? No problem. Maybe you will relate better to that concrete bridge you are about to drive across with your family during this summer's vacation road trip. It is certainly possible that the bridge looks just fine as you approach. Perfectly safe to drive upon. What if I told you that there was no rebar in that concrete structure? Are you still willing to drive across with your family? My vision for this book is to provide the rebar prior to construction of your leadership bridge that connects you to your people to not only make it safe for generations to come, but awe inspiring as well.

Will you still have work to do when your reading is finished? Absolutely! Filling in the rest of the puzzle, paving and lining the road surface of the bridge—however you want to look at it, you will still have work to do. But at least after reading this book, and adopting these core values, you will have a solid structure upon which to build.

The interviews that follow addressing commitment, trust, caring and the Leadership Spotlight comprise what I believe are the four all-important corner pieces of the puzzle. Those are the core values required of any effective and inspirational leader. Also included are discussions about two additional topics, the importance of identifying and committing to your mission as well as the all-important principle of self-leadership. As you read those chapters, you will see why those are also included in a conversation about leadership fundamentals. When you begin to see an interaction between the principles, you will have aggressively begun your journey to become a more effective and inspirational leader.

As a side note, I have not numbered the chapters. That is not an oversight. It is important to realize that the chapters and the contents within all carry equal weight, with one chapter no more important than the other.

RICHARD BROWN

COMMITMENT

"Mission first, Marines always!"

—Colonel John W. Ripley, USMC

*"Every leader has some moment in which
their subordinates will be able to look at
them and know if there is that kind of
commitment."*

—Colonel David Dotterrer, USMC (ret.)

RICHARD BROWN

The significance of a leader demonstrating commitment to the those that they lead cannot be understated. When I refer to commitment, here is my frame of reference. To me, "commitment" reflects the **drive** to accomplish a mission **regardless** of the obstacles present. Commitment is in an entirely different league than involvement. "Involvement" is exhibited by a **desire** to accomplish the mission, **depending** on the obstacles that are present.

In the leadership experience, it is easy to understand and comprehend the importance of

21

your commitment to accomplish your objective. Just as critical is your commitment to look out for the welfare of those that you lead. These two principles are inseparable to the effective as well as inspirational leader.

Leaders are not born as leaders. They are made into leaders over time, through study, experience, the influence of others, and a willingness to adopt and change one's own behavior. I am convinced that there is no leadership gene on the DNA double helix. Leadership is not instinctive.

My first interview is with a retired Marine Corps colonel. I will admit that Colonel David Dotterer has been responsible for just a bit of the self-doubt I have battled regarding that belief, but I am still convinced of the inherent truth that leadership is a learned skill.

From my first exposure as a freshman to "Dot", as he was called by those with more self-confidence than I, at the Naval R.O.T.C. quonset hut at Oregon State University, I have wondered WHEN his leadership ability began to develop. Surely, shortly after his birth, young David was inspiring those sharing the maternity ward with him to cry only at only their appointed hours, so that everyone could get the sleep required by newborns. At least that is the impression he gave me, as well as my class of fellow freshman midshipman. Being able to observe him until his commissioning as a second lieutenant served as an example of what we should strive for in our own development.

Colonel Dotterrer could certainly be featured as the first interview in his own right but I have chosen to begin with Dave for a different reason. We both had the good fortune to be exposed to a level of leadership and principle few people get a chance to witness first-hand. That experience took place at a time in our development as leaders and officers of Marines that was beyond impactful and bordering on life changing.

As midshipman, we were both led and mentored by an individual by the name of John Ripley. A young major when we first made his acquaintance, Major Ripley would become a Marine Corps legend as the result of his heroism in Vietnam. His exploits can be read in his Navy Cross citation following this introduction. While Colonel Ripley's leadership has been the subject of two books, *"The Bridge at Dong Ha"* and *"American*

Knight," that is not my purpose for discussing him in this book. I have chosen to feature Colonel Ripley to bring life to the concept of commitment. Colonel Ripley was given a mission that not only seemed impossible, but was certain to cause him to "die in place" in attempting its successful completion. Despite incredible obstacles, he would not only achieve his objective, but survive as well due to nothing more than his own superhuman drive and commitment.

Colonel Ripley is no longer with us, so I have asked Colonel Dotterer to reflect on his experience as a young Marine officer being trained by and serving with Colonel Ripley. As you read his comments, bear in mind that I witnessed a significant degree of mutual respect between Colonel Ripley, and the young, green "Candidate Dotterer." That speaks volumes about both individuals.

The President of the United States in the name of the Congress takes pleasure in presenting the

NAVY CROSS
to
CAPTAIN JOHN W. RIPLEY

UNITED STATES MARINE CORPS

The President of the United States of America takes pleasure in presenting the Navy Cross to Captain John W. Ripley (MCSN: 0-84239), United States Marine Corps, for extraordinary heroism on 2 April 1972 while serving as the Senior Marine Advisor to the Third Vietnamese Marine Corps Infantry Battalion in the Republic of

Vietnam. Upon receipt of a report that a rapidly moving, mechanized, North Vietnamese army force, estimated at reinforced divisional strength, was attacking south along Route #1, the Third Vietnamese Marine Infantry Battalion was positioned to defend a key village and the surrounding area. It became imperative that a vital river bridge be destroyed if the overall security of the northern provinces of Military Region One was to be maintained. Advancing to the bridge to personally supervise this most dangerous but vitally important assignment, Captain Ripley located a large amount of explosives which had been pre-positioned there earlier, access to which was blocked by a chain-link fence. In order to reposition the approximately 500 pounds of explosives, Captain Ripley was obliged to reach up and hand-walk along the beams while his body dangled beneath the bridge. On five separate occasions, in the face of constant enemy fire, he moved to points along the bridge and, with the aid of another advisor who pushed the explosives to him, securely emplaced them. He then detonated the charges and destroyed the bridge, thereby stopping the enemy assault. By his heroic actions and extraordinary courage, Captain Ripley undoubtedly was instrumental in saving an untold number of lives.

His inspiring efforts reflected great credit upon himself, the Marine Corps, and the United States Naval Service

www.freerepublic.com/fuxus.news/28668/replies?c=83

RICHARD BROWN

COLONEL DAVID G. DOTTERRER
USMC (Ret)

Colonel David D. Dotterrer grew up in Eugene, Oregon. In 1973, he graduated from Oregon State University and received his commission in the United States Marine Corps through the R.O.T.C. program.

Colonel Dotterrer first joined the 3rd Marine Division in Okinawa, Japan where he served as an infantry platoon commander. He participated in Operation Frequent Wind, the evacuation of Saigon.

Colonel Dotterrer subsequently served as an infantry company commander with the 2nd Marine

Division in Camp Lejeune, North Carolina, as the Marine Officer Instructor at the University of Washington R.O.T.C. unit, with the United Nations Command in Seoul, Korea, and at Headquarters Marine Corps in Washington, D.C.

In addition to his infantry platoon and company commands, he has commanded the 1ˢᵗ Air Naval Gunfire Liaison Company in Camp Pendleton, California and Marine Barracks, Washington, D.C.

He is a graduate of the Army Command and General Staff College and the Naval War College and holds Masters degrees in Military History and National Security and Strategic Studies. Most recently he served as the military assistant to the Secretary of the Navy.

Colonel Dotterrer retired in January 2001 with 27 years of service as a Marine and currently resides in Ashland, Oregon.

Since retiring from the Marine Corps, Colonel Dotterrer served from 2011 to 2014 as the Budget Coordinator and Strategic Analyst in the Oregon Legislature for the Republican House and Senate Caucuses.

Colonel Dotterrer is married to the Kerry Dotterrer, (Roberts) of Ashland, Oregon. They have two children, Charles and Stephanie. Charles is a Marine officer currently serving in Iraq as a rifle company commander.

RICHARD BROWN

Richard: Colonel, I can't tell you what a great honor it is to interview you regarding Colonel John W. Ripley! I would also like to express my appreciation for the perspectives that you are willing to share regarding leadership and commitment as the result of your exposure to the colonel.

Col. Dotterrer: Oh, it's an honor to talk about Colonel Ripley, When he arrived at Oregon State University from Vietnam, you and I were already pretty established there as a midshipman officers. Now, just to explain to our readers, at the time Major Ripley was faculty, and we were students. He was also on active duty, serving as an instructor. He was a recent Navy Cross recipient in Vietnam who would become a Marine Corps legend. I was the senior midshipman at Oregon State Navy R.O.T.C. We had a very accomplished Marine in his own right, Major Mike Sweeney who was in the position of which Major Ripley went on to assume.

Richard: I'm curious as to what your expectations were when you first heard that Major Sweeney was going to be leaving, to be replaced by this captain, or this new major, who was going to be coming in and taking over the Marine Instructor position at Oregon State.

Col. Dotterrer: Well, my impression was this. First, during the Spring of 1972, before Major Ripley showed up, Major Sweeney–whom all of us worshipped as a tremendous leader came into the class and said; "Captain John Ripley is going to be my replacement. He is currently in Vietnam and here's what's going on." We knew that this legend was showing up and Mike Sweeney made no bones about it. He would say "I feel very good about this. You're going to be getting a legend to the making. A tremendous leader is going to be taking my place and here's what you need to know about him." So, that was the set up that we had. Those of us who were juniors would go off to Officer Candidate School (OCS) that summer. We went through the crucible of OCS, which is one of the most difficult things you will ever do in your life. For most of us, it was our very first exposure to the "real" United States Marine Corps. I came back to Oregon in early August, about a month before school started, and I was the fall term midshipman in command, meaning I was the senior midshipman in the battalion. I lived in Eugene, Oregon, which was 40 miles away from Oregon State. When I returned home, I thought I should introduce myself to the new Major; which I did.

As I said, I had just come out of Officer Candidate School when I made that visit to Oregon State. Of course, things were very quiet because it was still summer, and he had just checked in a couple of weeks before. He was just beginning to get his feet on the ground.

As I walked in to introduce myself, he looks up at me and says: "Well, okay candidate!" I don't know if you remember that but he referred to all of us as "candidates" until we received our commission upon graduation. He asked, "What are you doing at noon today?" I said "Well, nothing sir." He said "Good, if you have your running gear with you, let's go run!" I thought "That's an interesting way to start a conversation." I was impressed, he really was a take-charge guy.

As a graduate of the Naval Academy, although he had been a midshipman, Major Ripley knew very little about how Navy R.O.T.C. would run. Unlike the Naval Academy midshipmen, you are not often at sea, you are a full-time college student at a regular college and a part-time midshipman. You go to classes and you only put on your uniform one day a week. He came out of the Naval Academy into an environment in which you were a midshipman 24/7. What was impressive about him was he clearly knew where he wanted to go in terms of leadership, but he also understood that he was in a different environment than the one in which he had gone to school. He was very interested in sitting down with me and saying "Okay, talk to me about how the battalion here at Oregon State works as opposed to the midshipmen and battalion at the Naval Academy. There is a lot of crossover but there are a lot of differences." It was very impressive.

We would go back and forth. It was a great symbiotic relationship. I understood how he wanted to run it, and he understood how the midshipman battalion ran and how I wanted to run my part of it. He also understood how Marine units and how active duty Navy units ran and how you can blend all those pieces together to make sure that we were graduating and commissioning the readiest Navy and Marine officer. He was quite open to changes that I suggested. I can tell you he had high standards, and he was a hard charger and a hard worker, but you know there was nothing that was overbearing; you weren't intimidated by him, you were just impressed by him.

Richard: It seems like he was effective at taking a group of midshipmen, who were certainly interested in being involved, and converting them into a committed group of midshipmen, more like the Naval Academy. Would you say that was accurate?

Col. Dotterer: Yes, that is right, and it was interesting. I think most of us understood that a leader who has an expectation of you—that leader will consciously and unconsciously communicate that expectation. Your good workers, or your good Marines or your good sailors will all pick up on that. Immediately they'll follow. It was one of those implicit and explicit kinds of things in terms of commitments that he expected, but you knew that he was committed. Just as importantly, you understood that he expected you to be committed to becoming the best junior officer you could be. When I think back to it, although there were some exclusive times where you could talk about things, most of that was inclusive communicated leadership by example. Leadership by expectation. You just knew that was expected of you and therefore you did it.

Richard: Colonel Ripley's exploits at the bridge of Dong Ha (as described at the beginning of this chapter) earned him this nation's second highest award for valor in combat, the Navy Cross. Would you relate to me some of your insights on the events of Dong Ha as it has related to your own command experience during your career in the Marine Corps?

Col. Dotterrer: Later in my career, approximately seven years after I received my commission, Captain Dotterer showed up at Camp Lejeune for assignment to an infantry battalion. My orders directed me to one battalion, but after I checked with the division, they said, "We have had a request and you are instead going First Battalion, Second Marine Regiment." I said, "Oh really? Well, who's the Commander over there?" They replied, "Lieutenant Colonel Ripley."

This is now my second introduction to the man. He's now a Lieutenant Colonel and he greeted me with "Hi Dave, how you doing? Haven't seen you for a while!" I was thrilled to be under his command once again. When I look back and see the commitment he expected of us as midshipmen and then, seeing that he expected the same commitment from the Marines in his battalion, it all makes sense. That expectation was implicit. Everybody knew he was committed because they knew of his brave act at the bridge. He never really talked about it, it's just that it was always there. You just thought "Okay Colonel, you don't have to prove this to me. "We know that you are committed."

Every leader has some moment in which their subordinates will be able to look at them and know if there is that kind of commitment. You don't have to earn a Navy Cross. You know you are committed to whatever organization you belong to and you would convey that as a leader. I'm committed, my expectations are that you'd be committed as well and here's how I am showing you I'm committed. Colonel Ripley was the ultimate expression of that. Most of us don't get a chance to earn a Navy Cross like he did, but that doesn't mean we can't show commitment.

Richard: Colonel Ripley has been quoted as saying "Mission first and Marines always." You get the impression from Colonel Ripley that his commitment to mission was above approach, particularly considering the events at Dong Ha. I'm certain my experience with him confirms that, as does yours. On a related topic, what about commitment to the Marine's welfare? How does that relate to commitment to mission in your mind and in your experience?

Col. Dotterrer: Well, in the military services, and certainly in the Marine Corps, you do have something that needs to be understood and accepted. Obviously, your mission does come first, because that's why you are there. Some will say there's conflict between conducting your mission and taking care of your Marines.

If you really wanted to say "Look, I'm only going to take care of my Marines," you wouldn't send them on a dangerous mission in the first place. You understand that war is a very dangerous endeavor, but you know what? Every leader faces those kinds of issues, and you must blend them. I think his idea of "mission first" is critical. That is why the organization exists. But that certainly doesn't say it all. It only says part of it.

You also need to keep your Marines, or whoever it is you are leading, in mind because you won't accomplish your mission without them. It's a blending, and sometimes it's a balancing act. But what he's saying is that the two, mission and welfare, are not in conflict. They are something that you must balance. You must work with it and understand those commitments as a leader. The simple fact of the matter was that he made sure that we accomplished our mission at Oregon State, but at the same time, he took care of us.

Richard: Colonel, as you are aware, very few of our readers have spent any time in the military. It is reported that only seven percent of the American population has ever put on a uniform from any branch of the service. We have readers from many different walks of life. Thus, it is understandable that folks in the civilian world, in various types of different endeavors might say "This is military stuff and I wasn't a Marine, I'm not in the Army. It's different when you are in the military. This stuff doesn't really apply to me in the civilian world." Would you address that perspective?

Col. Dotterrer: Leadership is leadership, it doesn't matter where it is being applied. A good leader must adapt the fundamentals of leadership to the situation in which they find yourselves. Marine officers routinely find themselves in different situations.

Interestingly, for all those readers who are in business, I have a very good friend who is the retired CEO of a multibillion dollar corporation, He is also a Marine officer and he served in Vietnam and earned the Silver Star. He left the Marine Corps, got his MBA, entered the corporate world and is now retired. He told me that everything he learned as a young Marine officer about leadership, he could apply to his successful business career. He said "Yes, I had to adjust. I had to understand the situation is different but the basic leadership that I learned was still very applicable." That is how I would address that issue. Of course, there are different situations. That's the definition of being a good leader. Understanding the situation you are in and applying the fundamentals.

Richard: I'm going to ask you to sum this incredibly valuable discussion up with one other point. I'm working with individuals who have stepped into a leadership position for the very first time. They may be middle aged, they are in business environments, they are male and female, and they are thinking "Hmm! What do I do now that I'm a leader?" What advice would you give them to start out on the right foot?

Col. Dotterer: Well, I would say that you need to recognize that leadership is at it's very fundamental core, a human endeavor. You are not a perfect human being nor are any of your subordinates. At the end of the day, leadership is about human interaction. It is about treating people with dignity and respect. Look to mission first to understand that the mission of whatever your organization is comes first. That's not in conflict with the idea of taking care of your subordinates. When I say, "Take care of your subordinates," remember they are expecting leadership from you. They are looking to you for leadership, and that's the way human beings are. Just understand that you are in a human interaction environment and you need to adjust to work with that environment with high expectations. Take care of the people working for you, treat them with dignity and respect, and you'll find a lot of other things will take care of themselves.

MISSION

*"You can't take a person's
innate personality traits,
strengths, gifts, and talents,
and paint on them something to try
to make them what they're not."*

*"Effective teachers are servant leaders.
They are there to serve the needs of the
kids. That's what makes effectiveness.
Caring more about the needs of who is in
the audience than performance or
whatever up in front."*

—Connie Schroeder Grosse

RICHARD BROWN

Just as a group of people without an objective isn't much more than a happy hour, leadership without a clearly defined mission is simply irritating. Simple math—a topic rarely attributed to my next contributor—would state what appears to be the obvious when it comes to commitment: to lead people, give them an objective and make them want to commit to accomplishing it. Like any good advanced math problem, there is another factor that must be included in that equation.

While commitment to accomplish the mission is important if one is to become an effective leader, commitment to the development and welfare of your people is required as well if one desires to reach beyond effective to become inspirational. One glance at the bio of Connie Schroeder Grosse will provide a stellar example of a teacher who embraced commitment to her mission of teaching as well as to the welfare of her students in rock star fashion.

Having known Connie for over 40 years, I have the privilege of being one of her many Facebook friends. It is here that one can see the true impact that she has had on her students. Even in retirement, Connie continues to be more than just a teacher of chemistry. She also enthusiastically embraced her additional duties as mentor, friend, example, and cheerleader for their success. The praise, gratitude and love professed to "Mrs. Grosse" comes through loud and clear from comments posted by her students to this day.

It is my great pleasure to introduce you to Connie Schroeder Grosse, and to let you sit in on our conversation regarding the missions involved in effective and inspirational lead

CONNIE SCHROEDER GROSSE

THE TEACHER YOU WISH YOU AND YOUR KIDS HAD IN HIGH SCHOOL

After having graduated from the University of California at Davis in 1973 with a Bachelor's degree in chemistry, I earned my teaching credential and became a teacher at El Dorado High School. A Golden Hawk from 1974 until 2013, I taught three levels of chemistry and physics during my tenure. I served as the Department Chair for the science department for 30 years and was engaged in many, many school activities, coaching athletic teams, and serving in leadership positions at both the school and district level. Over the years, I also enjoyed writing and contributing to numerous high school and college chemistry textbooks and helping to develop an innovative chemistry web site. In 1988 I was extremely honored to be selected Orange County Teacher of the Year. In 1999 I was named one of three recipients of the Presidential Excellence in Math and Science Teaching award for the state of California.

I loved every day of being a science teacher and was blessed to work with a group of amazing, stimulating, talented colleagues. I thoroughly enjoyed developing creative and challenging lessons for students, helping them better understand the phenomenal natural world they live in, and equipping them for the challenges of their future goals and aspirations. I never met a student who couldn't learn, and I was inspired to give my best to every student, every day, whatever it took.

Author's note: To any of my readers who lived through the 1960's, you may have wondered what ever happened to Gidget, the character played by Sally Field in the television show of the same name. I remember her as the cute, perky surfer girl occupying most of my early teen daydreams. I am proud to announce that she became a high school teacher in Orange County. Folks, meet Gidget!

Richard: I'd like to take you back just a couple of years if you don't mind. Back to your time as a student teacher or as you were wrapping up your education and find out who was it that made you want to be a teacher.

Connie: It is interesting that it has probably not gotten easier to answer that question. As the years have gone by, people ask me that every now and again. Let me approach it this way. When I was young, I had the seed of the idea that I might like to be a teacher. There was just something that was planted in me. I think a lot of it had to do with growing up in a family with a father who was a teacher.

More important even then him being a formal classroom teacher was the fact that I was lucky enough to grow up with a mom and a dad who loved to take all of us kids on summer vacations. They just taught us wherever we were. We loved to explore. Lots of road trips. Lots of things out in nature. Lots of historical things. I grew up with parents who loved to just embrace this idea of teaching their kids things. I think that really planted the seed in me.

Ironically enough, I was one of those kids who came out of high school liking everything. I liked learning. I was easily fascinated by all sorts of things. I didn't really feel as though I were destined for a particular career path.

My dad, who had been a teacher for most of his career, was really kind of discouraging. It's funny to think about that now. He had seen changes in educational policy as well as sociological changes that impacted schools and so on. He was kind of discouraging to my siblings and I about teaching. He said, "Dream a little bit bigger than that or think about something different such as medical school or some other kind of profession."

I look back, and out of the five children in the family, four of us became teachers. I always say his life spoke louder than his words. Honestly, if I do a little self-assessment, I think I became a teacher because I have always loved to understand ideas and to explain what I understand to others. There's just that little seed.

Richard: The effect that parents have on us whether they know they are having that effect or not is interesting.

As you were developing as a teacher what sort of guidance did you get from your instructors at the time in terms of what the ultimate mission of a teacher should be?

Connie: That also is a really interesting and challenging question for me. It turns out just this fall I began teaching a class to potential teachers at a local university. It's so funny because I think back in my mind to the bad rap that college classes in education preparation often have. So much theory about what teaching is or what teaching isn't and so on. Yet every aspect of what I learned was valuable. I look back on my life and see every course, every word, every piece of advice as somehow playing a part in painting a picture for me as a teacher.

The absolute best example, the absolute best training is on-the-job training and just watching good teachers teach. There's nothing like it. That is a really valuable thing for young teachers to do. Rather than theorizing too much about what they should be, first year teachers are best served by just watching good teachers do their thing. To see both the art and the science of teaching. Both the technique and the magic that happens in a classroom.

In my student teaching experience I had the best of both worlds. I was assigned to two different master teachers. Of those two teachers I had, one dictated to me what I should do. He was very "toe the mark." He had schedules. He had organization. He wanted me, as his young protege, to fall right in line with the way that he did things. If he felt a certain way about organization, I should feel that way about organization. If he felt like he could cover so much during a class session, then I should be able to cover that much during a class session. From him I learned the idea of mission from the point of view of setting a goal and achieving something. That's very important in the classroom. I believe in many respects, that for a teacher, there's nothing more important than the stewardship that I have over those fifty minutes, over those thirty kids. What can I do to make the most out of it? The idea of a mission accomplishing something is very important.

On the other hand, my other master teacher was the most loving, gracious and generous leader, mentor and shaper of me. Though he gave me guidelines for what I should be teaching, he really gave me free rein to be as creative and as different from him as I wanted to be. That's a scary and risky postion for a teacher to take, but I am so thankful for that as well.

My mission is to accomplish things. I'm a very-goal oriented person, so that appeals to me. On the other hand, I love to create lessons and to think of stories. I love to use examples and to develop things on my own. The idea of the second master teacher telling me that I wasn't ever going to be a good teacher, much less a great teacher until I learned to be my own good teacher, my own great teacher, helped me learn to use my own creative gifts. That really was the icing on the cake.

Richard: So the first master teacher taught their own way and the second master teacher taught in really a different way. Was one more effective than the other?

Connie: I think effectiveness in teaching is a really interesting topic. I think different teachers can be effective in many different ways. A lot of it stems from the personality of the teacher in the various contexts. In other words, you can't take a person's personality traits, strengths, gifts and talents and paint onto them something to try to make them what they're not. That is one of the most amazing and important keys in teaching and maybe in most professions, careers, callings. The innate gifts and talents that I have dictate what kind of teacher or what kind of professional I will be. I hesitate to say one was more effective than the other.

You can probably think of teachers that you connected with more on some kind of visceral level. Who knows exactly why? There are just certain people who seem to be more effective for different kinds of kids. I've seen lots of teachers, from straight laced to very flexible. Both were very effective.

Richard: One of the things we teach in our leadership class is that there are different styles of leadership. There is a democratic style, a delegative style and an autocratic style. Examining Mother Teresa, you see a woman who was a tremendous leader. Look at George Patton, also a tremendous leader. They were both effective with their own individual style .

Connie: I think what makes teachers effective, regardless of the style or personality, is the bottom line that effective teachers are servant leaders. They are there to serve the needs of the kids. That's effectiveness. Caring more about the needs of who is in the audience than performance up in front.

Richard: The depth of that statement is profound. Depending on how effectiveness is defined, whether it is task accomplishment or some other measure, I would even take it a step farther and say that servant leadership, caring about those students beyond the curriculum, is what makes a teacher beyond effective and reaches towards inspirational. The type of teacher students remember twenty years later. The type of teacher who has former students popping up on Facebook saying, "Mrs. Gross, I can't tell you how much you meant to me."

In our discussion prior to this interview, you mentioned the concept of "The game is over." At the end of the year you put everything back in the box in May as the school year ended. Your game was over for that year. Right around September or the middle of August, you would start getting ready for the next year. You would open the box again for really a whole new game because you would have a whole new group of students. How did you go about setting a mission for the year, not knowing what sort of students you were going to have? You had no idea what their strengths were or what their challenges were. How did you identify your new mission?

Connie: That is a wonderful question! I'm going to start with a little bit of a story because this is what cames to mind when you first asked that question of me.

One of the things that schools are required to do, as they should be, on a regular basis every six years or so is to go through an accreditation process. Outside panels of educators come into a school and investigate, observe, and chat with everybody on campus to assess how well the school is accomplishing what the school is meant to be accomplishing. That means both curricularly and getting kids prepared for what comes after high school. I'm sure any teachers out there know what I'm talking about.

One of the things that schools will often do is to draft a mission statement for the school. We want to make sure that people understand that we're really reaching out and caring about all kinds of kids. Sometimes these mission statements can get almost funny. Let me give you an example. I won't name the school but here's a mission statement I found online. This particular school "Will provide students with the necessary skills and knowledge to become lifelong learners, effective communicators and socially productive citizens who are prepared for life choices and challenges in a global society." Now that is a beautifully worded, all-inclusive kind of mission statement that I get lost in.

The last accreditation our school went through was under new leadership. We had a wonderful leader who was taking us through this process. He said to keep it simple. What are we trying to accomplish, regardless of who our audience is, how adept the kids are that particular year, how mature they are when they come into us, what kind of parental involvement there will be, what kind of needs are we really trying to fulfill? So our mission statement became simply "Equipping students for success." The subtext of that, which was provided by this new assistant principal was simply this; "Every student, every day, whatever it takes."

When I remove myself from my mission statement being about what I have to teach to a mission to equip students, the whole perspective shift helps me understand something. No matter who I get walking into my class. If I have a bunch of students or a small class, mature students or an immature class, kids with a lot of background in science, kids with very little math skills, whatever it may be, I see that mission statement "Every student, every day, whatever it takes; equipping students for success." That dictates to me how I will approach each lesson. The curriculum that I cover may not be much different. In fact, it is really repetitious in terms of the concepts that I want kids to be able to solve and so on. My approach, my structure, the avenues that I use to teach will depend upon who that audience is that sits in front of me. It's all about them. It's not about me—it's all about them.

Richard: The mission statement you just shared, "Every student, every day, whatever it takes" gives me chills and it makes my voice break a little bit. It really makes me want to cross out of some of these next couple of questions. What I see in that mission statement is the need to adapt to the situation that is present in the classroom. As opposed to saying "Here is my mission, now I'll go meet my kids," it is "I'm going to go meet my kids and we're going to get accomplished what we need to get accomplished in order to develop them."

So many times people get wrapped up in the first mission statement you gave. I saw a mission statement the other day similar to the one you mentioned. I was reading it and I had the same reaction. I consider myself a fairly intelligent individual. I'm reading this mission and I don't know what it means. I think any organization that's trying to achieve something that doesn't have an understandable, relevant mission statement is lost. It is almost like trying to find your way on the hike when you don't know where you are going.

The other thing I see are mission statements that get written, and then, get put in a annual report or they get put away for the year. "Okay, here's the mission statement. See you next year." What the leader is trying to accomplish may very well be in opposition to the mission statement.

Then there is this concept that a mission statement is akin to the Ten Commandments being handed down on the mountaintop. They can't be changed, which is a mistake. The mission statement of "Every student, every day, whatever it takes" is perfect because it allows you to do whatever it takes. It's not "these are the behaviors that need to be adapted," it's "whatever it takes."

Connie, you make a very clear point about establishing the mission at the beginning of the school year to accomplish what you want to accomplish. Have you ever seen an example where situations change maybe mid-execution and it becomes a necessity to adjust that mission?

Connie: I think it happens all the time. In fact I think a good teacher is constantly changing in small ways and sometimes in big ways. I'm always adjusting to make the message fit the listener in the most effective way possible. My favorite example of adjusting the mission to needs is related to one of my best friends. I had the privilege of teaching with Carol for probably fifteen or twenty years. She is just about ready to retire as well. Her commitment to kids at school is just a beautiful thing to see. For many years she taught with me in the science department. Her assignment was to teach kids in the entry level courses. She had a lot of students in her class who didn't necessarily like school, who didn't really see academic achievement as something that was a high calling in their lives. These kids were sometimes just little tough nuts to teach. They were not always the most likable or flexible kids either. She had to deal with some students who make teaching especially challenging.

For years she taught in a very traditional way because she felt that kind of structure was what the kids needed in terms of homework every night. The kids came into class and took notes every day. It was a very teacher-directed classroom. She was terrific about holding them accountable with attendance and that sort of thing. She was very effective and well-practiced. She demonstrated a lot of best practices in her classroom. One day she came over during an especially challenging year with students who just were not responding. She was in tears and she said to me, "Connie, I'm trying to accomplish something. I'm trying to teach but nobody is learning. I'm teaching in a way that I think I'm accomplishing something but I can tell the kids are not learning."

I was so excited when, early the next morning she said, "I did a whole new thing last night." Single-handedly she had revamped her entire curriculum. Rather than all that traditional structure and so on, she began to give kids experiences within the class period. They would take a little field trip outside the classroom around campus to learn biology. She developed an ecology study where they spent a number of days outside investigating everything they possibly could about the environment around school. She had kids work in groups. She talked with them about what they liked best in terms of the way they liked to learn.

It really empowered them to become more active students. It really changed the way she taught from that point on. Her heart was set on giving the kids what they needed. It necessitated a whole change and it was very successful. I'm really proud of her.

Richard: That's one of the most important things about a mission statement. First of all it should drive your behavior. But if you're not getting what you want to accomplish, you can't be afraid to either change your behavior or even change your mission.

Connie, as we begin to wrap this interview, I would like to ask you a question that goes beyond mission accomplishment. There are curriculua and there are the core subjects you are supposed to teach that you certainly accomplish, but from the standpoint of bringing value to that student's life, are there rewards beyond being able to check tasks off of the list?

Connie: That is such a great question and in fact it may be my favorite question because it lets me reflect back on my years of teaching. Looking back on thirty-nine years in the classroom there was nothing that overwhelmed me more than the notion that I had a chance to know thousands of kids with gifts, talents, foibles, challenges facing them, odds facing them and so on.

I frequently have a chance to bump into them and share a little life with them. I often think of the impact that kids had on my life. Shaping me, giving me hope, teaching me more about the world, giving me a sense of what this whole thing called life is. The impact of kids on my life was profoundly greater than whatever impact I probably had on them. I've just been awestruck by what kids have been able to accomplish in the field of science and specifically in the field of chemistry which I taught.

One of my former students is the division head of Gerontology at the University of California San Francisco at the medical school. She is someone for whom a calling in science gave her not only an opportunity but, boy oh boy, this is nothing I taught her, but she has just used her gifts magnificently. She is really having an impact in the medical community. So there are kids that yes, I look back and think "Wow, they really had the gift and the ability to use the chemistry that I taught."

Perhaps that got them to a different place in life but that's not the story.

The story is the number of kids that I have a chance to run into. Either they would drop by the classroom after they had graduated or they send me a little notes, give me a phone call or just come visit. Nowadays messages on Facebook or whatever let me know that chemistry really doesn't play a really important part in their lives beyond high school. They have just found a happy satisfying little niche in life. Maybe raising a family. Maybe being the coach of the neighborhood baseball or soccer team. Maybe owning a small business. Maybe moving to an entirely different part of the world. Just getting their life into some little niche that really brings satisfaction. Its very rewarding to see them "simply" raising a happy family. We actually housed a couple of former students this summer who live overseas and who work as missionaries who are teaching. It's just that kind of thing. Kids from every walk of life who find every walk of life and their future. Just to think that each one of those, in some way or another, imparted part of themselves to me is just overwhelming.

Richard: Connie, what you have just explained really shines a light on the rewards of servant leadership. As you mentioned, after the first five years you begin to realize this. Taking a look at the responsibilities of leadership can be intimidating, but what it's really all about are the rewards of leadership, particularly servant leadership. There are certainly many responsibilities but they pale in comparison to the rewards that come from fulfilling those responsibilities.

I would like to give you the opportunity to leave our audience with one last thought for someone stepping into a leadership position for the first time. Maybe they are stepping into teaching, coaching, business, parenting or whatever. Are there any pearls that you would like to give them that will hopefully take them through their career?

Connie: I think the only thing that that I can provide that resides in my heart and in my mind when I hear that question is something that I had mentioned a little bit earlier. Leadership is really a position of honor and servantship.

There is nothing more powerful in this world than servant leadership. Seeing yourself as somebody who is there to bring out the best in those they are working with. No one person can accomplish the job, but if I can accomplish the job of awakening a spirit and inspiration in somebody else, there are two of us, that person and me, both working towards a common goal. Serving to unlock the gifts that others have is important to me.

I have a couple of quotes referring to that concept. It really is something that's important to me. Not so long ago, I read a quote from General Patton; "Don't tell people how to do things. Tell them what you want and let them surprise you with their ingenuity." I powerfully believe in that. I believe one of the greatest gifts a leader gives is to paint a picture in a vision.

The other quote is by Antoine de Saint-Exupery: "If you want to build a ship, don't summon people to buy wood, prepare tools, distribute jobs and organize the work; teach people the yearning for the wide, boundless ocean." A teacher does a lot of gathering wood, dividing up work and making assignments. Any leader does. Not just a teacher, not just a leader in the classroom but far and away the best gift of a leader can give his or her people is a sense of what the major mission is. To yearn for something. To long to be the best they can be. To accomplish something that is well beyond me and to give those they serve the idea, "I can learn how to accomplish that."

TRUST

"Along the lines of transparency, it is necessary that when you find out that you've made a mistake, you come forward and say "I made a mistake. Now I need to fix it."

"I think it's important to recognize that individuals in leadership don't get recognized for awards because that individual does everything on his own on her own."

−Meg VanderLaan

RICHARD BROWN

Many of the more well-known tactics affiliated with leadership deal with the topic of trust:

"Set a good example."

"Live and lead with integrity"

"Don't ask anyone to do something that you haven't done or wouldn't do yourself."

All those tactics are designed to generate a feeling of trust in a leader that from time to time may be required to give an order without allowing for discussion or having the order questioned. While this is particularly true in a crisis, it may also apply to more mundane situations. Nevertheless, it is always critical for genuine trust to be present between all parties in a leadership relationship for the team to function effectively.

One of my favorite demonstrations is to display the fragility of trust with a blank piece of paper. Actions or words that deteriorate the trust between individuals are symbolized by crumpling that piece of paper into a ball. It is certainly possible to open the ball of paper up and flatten it out. But you will not easily be able to return it to its former, smooth, original state.

The individual featured in the next interview has made the creation of trust the primary mission in her career. As a corporate communications professional, it might appear that Meg VanderLaan's chief responsibility is to present a favorable image to the press and the public of her employer. While that is certainly important, she is adamant that she cannot accomplish her mission if she has not generated trust from the reporters she briefs, or the corporate executives that send her forward to communicate with the press.

I can assure you Meg's ascension up the corporate ladder in her career has been accomplished because of her commitment to the principle of generating trust from everyone with whom she interacts.

RICHARD BROWN

MEG VANDERLAAN

CORPORATE COMMUNICATIONS
CONSULTANT

Meg is a global marketing and communications executive and consultant with a passion for storytelling. Over her nearly 30-year career, she has used her insight and leadership in marketing, public relations and communications to help companies transform their brands and express their stories in multiple cultures, languages and countries. Her experience spans a broad spectrum, and whether it is directing marketing and communications programs for companies in the healthcare industry, dot-com start-ups at the turn of the 21st century or the technical manufacturing and engineering space, she takes complex subjects and comunicates about them in a simple, reliable way.

Richard: Meg, thanks so much for being willing to take some of your time from your hectic schedule to share your thoughts with us on trust.

Meg: Thanks Rick. I appreciate that. It's great to be talking about this subject. It is something near and dear to my heart given the background that I've had in the communications industry. It is something I live every day, although I guess we should all as leaders live this subject every day.

Richard: When I look at your background, and from what I know of your career, you have really spanned a gamut of experience. From college to various industries, ranging from health care to construction, you have had quite a variety of messages to communicate.

I'd like to take you back to Gannon University if you don't mind. You have a degree in communication arts and a very impressive list of honors including the outstanding senior academic award for excellence and an award for distinguished service. You were a high-powered graduate, but when you left school, you were still just a graduate. I'd like you tell me about your first big kid job out of college.

RICHARD BROWN

Meg: When I first graduated from Gannon, I was looking for an opportunity. At first I thought I was going to get into journalism. I decided I really wanted the opportunity to tell a story for a long term. Journalists tell stories very quickly and I wanted to work for a corporation to be able to tell a corporate story.

I happened to be introduced to an individual who ran a public relations firm in Ohio. He introduced me to one of his clients and I ended up working for that individual. I started with Blue Cross & Blue Shield of Ohio. When I first got out of school, it was very different from my college experience. When I was a student, I was very involved. I was an active participant in various activities. When I first started working after college, it was a desk job. It was a great learning experience, but it was very different from what I had been used to for the previous four years.

Richard: You mentioned that real life was much different from school and I imagine that is true for everyone who graduates from college. Can you tell us about any experiences you might have had regarding self-doubt on your future path, despite how successful you were in school?

Meg: Oh absolutely! I think that self-doubt is something that we all experience at every stage of our career. We must be able to make sure that we can talk through it with ourselves.

Starting this job, I knew nothing about health insurance. I knew nothing about health care. I knew how to communicate. I knew how to tell stories. I knew how to talk to people, how to take complicated issues and break them up into less complicated subjects, but I didn't understand health care. How could I explain this to somebody else if I couldn't even understand it myself?

I decided to approach my boss and ask, "Is there an opportunity to create a new program for our subscribers? As you know, health insurance has been very complicated. All the documents that you see when you review your health insurance are very legal in nature. They're very complex and it can be quite intimidating."

We started a program called "Understanding Your Benefits." We created posters for employers to use at their locations and we started explaining things like what a co-pay is. What is a deductible? What it would it mean to reach these levels for the year? It was really a fun program!

This was when I learned one of my favorite lessons. That lesson was in proofreading. I didn't proofread everything thoroughly and something went to press with the wrong phone number. These people were calling a phone number that was supposed to be to our benefits line and instead it went to a hotel in South Carolina.

Richard: You know, it could have been much worse!

Meg: Ha! I guess it could have been worse. But this was a small boutique hotel and it was a 1-800 number that the hotel had to pay for every time they had an incoming call. They were less than satisfied with that program. We managed to work it out and we paid their bill. That experience taught me an important lesson of how important it is to review your work. In the spirit of transparency, it is necessary that when you find out that you've made a mistake, you come forward and say "I made a mistake. Now I need to fix it."

Richard: That makes a great point as to how you can establish trust even after you have made that inevitable "earth-shaking" mistake.

You mentioned individuals that were helpful in assisting you in seeing some of the self-doubt issues. How were those individuals helpful in helping you find your level of confidence?

Meg: It was fun to be part of that community, so long ago back before the Internet. The Internet was getting off the ground. We didn't have computers at our desks. We had to build relationships. We had to rely on each other. I worked with a couple of individuals to were really excited about bringing a very new person into the process. They helped to mentor me, helped to explain things to me and helped to challenge me to make sure that I was reaching and exceeding what their expectations were. It was really my coworkers who provided such a foundation.

Richard: It is interesting that when I ask people who is the person that has had the greatest influence on them and why, probably eight times out of ten they talk about being tested. They tell stories about being stretched and being developed by an individual who was their leader. They speak about how they could trust that person to know that what they were asking of them is something that they could achieve.

One of the first points we make regarding the assumption of a leadership role is that the individuals who are tasking us with that role know that we have what it takes to get the job done. We may not know everything, but they're willing to trust us. Even when we make mistakes, they give us the ability to demonstrate we can be trusted.

When I was looking at your resume I noticed that it wasn't long before you found yourself as a vice president of public relations. You were representing your employer's image in front of industry as well as the general population. At that point did you appreciate that you were being asked to balance transparency while avoiding the release of proprietary information?

Meg: Absolutely. In the role I occupied I represented the company every day. You are looking to talk about a scenario or share information about the company. You must have a very balanced approach. There is information that might be trade secrets to the company. There might be information that is confidential. It's very important as you're sharing information to be truthful and recognizing that there are circumstances where you are not at liberty to share information. Maybe it's a personnel issue. Maybe it's a private family matter. Maybe it's a company confidential scenario that you are not at liberty to share.

You certainly can be respectful. You recognize that the individuals who are seeking the information, journalists, have a job to do. They're looking to report news. They're looking for information. You act very respectfully. That's one of the principles that I have. I always return calls. I always return e-mail. Sometimes, I'm not at liberty to say anything and I very clearly state that. I think that is so much better than not returning a call and not respecting the individual who's asking the question. They're doing their job and they're doing what they need to do. At the same time being truthful is very important and if I can't say anything then I'll tell you I can't say anything. If I tell you a company needs to adjust the way that it goes forward, then we talk about that. If there is a situation where the company hasn't been involved in any wrongdoing or hasn't made a mistake, then certainly I'll be stating that as well. Being very clear about where the company stands is important.

Richard: That's very interesting because in my limited perspective on public relations and corporate voice, I can see very clearly the need to be able to trust what is coming from the podium if I were reporter. But I hear what you're saying. Trust goes more than one direction. Not only do the individuals in the audience, in front of your podium, need to know they can trust what you're telling them is the straight scoop. But the individuals in the back of the room, the people that have put you behind that podium need to know that they will be able to trust you to maintain a confidence. You must not only present a good corporate image but protect proprietary information as well, so it's a real balancing act wouldn't you say?

Meg: It definitely is a balancing act. It is also not just the trust from the company but the trust from the reporters. I must build relationships with the media as well. I need to understand that what I'm telling them is going to appear in print or on the Web or the evening news in the form that I have delivered it to them. It's a total balancing act and it's a total act of trust all the way around.

I have had circumstances where I have had very good relationships with reporters. We've built a relationship where they contact me when they hear something or want more information. They know that I'll contact them when I know something is happening or we have a big announcement and I'm ready to share the information. I will make a personal phone call. I will send a personal e-mail and say, "Let's talk."

Richard: I want to progress now into a discussion on delegation and trusting other people to do things that may be unconventional, yet work out for the best. People whose approach might not have been the norm but worked out well nevertheless.

Meg: One of the things that my team always joked about is the fact that every time I decide to take vacation, a crisis hits. We work very hard during times when there are no crisis situations to prepare for those times. We make sure that everybody understands what protocol is and what we need to do. I am grateful for the opportunity to have individuals in the company who recognize that some of these opportunities are wonderful for public relations. It's not always about crisis. It's opportunities to tell our story to the public.

Sometime the opportunities I bring forward are not conventional opportunities at all. One case was around a convention several years ago, when the Democratic National Convention was coming to Denver. I approached the C.E.O. of the company and said "We have been asked by the executive producer of N.B.C. News to host the N.B.C. News team on our campus. We are right downtown. We are very close to where the Democratic National Convention is going to be held. The N.B.C. News crew thought this would be the perfect place to be close to the venue. We would be showcasing the downtown Denver skyline and really showcasing and highlighting what Denver has to offer."

The company I was working for at the time was not a business-to-consumer company. It was a business-to-business company. At first glance you could say "Well how is this going to be good publicity for us? How is this going to help us grow our business?" If you look at that in a very traditional sense you would have to say that it's not. These individuals are not going to be buying what we're selling. We're not a hotel or a restaurant. We're not in this to grow our business right now, but if you look at it from the standpoint of publicity, it really is an opportunity. Look at it from the perspective of a good corporate citizen. We are increasing the recognition of our name, of our brand. We're hosting the individuals who are here to highlight not only the convention but what we're all about.

We did end up hosting them. We had them set up in a double-decker stage in our parking lot. We hosted the talent, the crew and the producers. It was one of the most fun experiences I've had in my career because it was unconventional. It was an opportunity to say that "publicity doesn't have to be traditional." It was very rewarding to the company as well.

RICHARD BROWN

Richard: Just a few weeks ago you received an honor from the Business Marketing Association of Colorado naming you the Business Marketer of the Year. You are also considered one of the top twenty-five most powerful women in Colorado by the Colorado Women's Chamber of Commerce. That's impressive, but knowing you, it's not surprising at all. To what do you attribute these honors?

Meg: I've had a lot of fun over the last year and I've had the opportunity to work with an incredible team. I think it's important to recognize that individuals in leadership don't get recognized for awards because that individual does everything on his own on her own. This past year I've had the opportunity to work with this team on a very unique and important project.

Through this kind of unconventional approach that I have towards public relations, I worked with producers in Los Angeles who put together a documentary about some of the work the company I work for was doing at the Panama Canal. The producers worked very hard to tell the story of the engineering marvels that we were undertaking at the canal. They approached the History Channel and this story became a "Modern Marvel" special on the Panama Canal which aired in 2015. All the accolades that I have recently received were based on the work that I have done over the last twelve months.

That was another opportunity within the company to come forward and say "We have this great story to tell. Even though we are not a business-to-consumer company, we are a business-to-business company." The general audience of the History Channel is not necessarily going to be the decision-maker who decides to hire us as a company, but it might be. It might be the future decision-maker or it might be a future or current employee who takes incredible pride in working for an organization that is working on such an enormous project, such an important project. It's been very exciting and I have my team to thank for that.

Richard: Somehow, I didn't expect any different kind of an answer from you, giving the credit to the team. That's really what it all comes down to. Ironically, none of those achievements would have ever occurred had someone not been willing to trust an individual who had an unconventional approach to accomplishing the mission.

Meg, this has been an incredible interview. I really appreciate it. From the standpoint of bringing some perspectives on trust, that was my goal, and you have really provided some tremendous insights, not only from a personal standpoint but also from a perspective of corporate communications, credibility, and teamwork.

CARING

"You know when you are in the presence of people with passion and expertise and they really care about you. They push you to levels that normally you would not think that you could achieve on your own. "

"We use servant leadership; a Christian view of leadership where first will be last and last will be first. I take care of my troops. I make sure that I'm trying to serve the people that I have. I didn't come to be served but to serve."

—Mike Lynch

RICHARD BROWN

There are a few specific situations in life that are ideal if you want to learn about a person. Marriage is obviously one of those but that process should be well underway prior to the vows. Sharing a foxhole in combat will do it, but how often do we get that opportunity in the business world? Rooming with a colleague at a business meeting is a real-world example of this process that immediately comes to mind. That how I got to know my next guest.

For close to five years in the corporate environment, Mike Lynch and I were assigned as roommates at quarterly sales meetings. While we might have talked sports during the down times in our room, he is a soccer fanatic. I'm a baseball guy, so that went nowhere fast. What we did have in common was leadership and coaching, and we discussed both topics for hours on end. Because of that interaction, we became friends. We spent considerable time hiking 30 miles on the Colorado Trail with my family during annual summer weekends. You can easily guess what our topics of discussion were above treeline. You learn a lot about a person at 12,000 feet in the wilderness with a 40-pound pack on your back during an approaching thunderstorm.

Mike has a passion for leading as a soccer coach as well as a person that is on par with his incredible passion for the game itself. His interview will acquaint you with how that came to be. Suffice to say that had any of my children developed any affinity for soccer at all, or if Mike had seen the light to take his skill as a coach to the beautiful past-time of baseball, there would be no one I would rather have coach them than Mike Lynch. Once you read his interview, and if you have aspiring young soccer players of your own, you **will** want to find out where he currently is coaching.

MIKE LYNCH

HEAD COACH, WOMEN'S SOCCER
BELMONT ABBEY COLLEGE

From emphasizing individual technique and ball control to teaching self-discipline, leadership and virtue, Proverbs 22:6, "Train the young in the way they should go; even when old, they will not swerve from it." (New American Bible) has been at the core of Mike Lynch's coaching philosophy for three decades. Lynch played college soccer at the United States Air Force Academy, serving as team captain and earning all-league and all-region accolades. He earned the US Soccer Federation National "A" Coaching license in 1992 and the

RICHARD BROWN

NSCAA "Premier" Diploma and US Soccer Federation National "Youth" Coaching license in 2010.

Prior to his current appointment as the head women's soccer coach at Belmont Abbey College, Coach Lynch held head coaching stints at Nebraska Wesleyan and Truman State Universities, plus an assistant coaching position at the United States Air Force Academy. Coach Lynch has also been heavily involved in youth soccer including the Olympic Development Program (ODP) and select club soccer teams in Ohio, Colorado, Missouri, Nebraska, and North Carolina. In addition to his soccer coaching profession, Lynch also served as an officer in the United States Air Force and worked as a manager in the healthcare industry for pharmaceutical giant, Pfizer, Inc. Lynch is married and has three children. He and his family love most anything outdoors. An avid runner until undergoing bilateral hip resurfacing surgeries, Lynch has completed several marathons, including the Boston Marathon in 2004.

Richard: Mike, first of all I'd like to talk to you about your extensive exposure to and experiences with leadership. You grew up in an Air Force family. Your father was an Air Force legend. Everything you have told me about him documents that he was a leader of the highest calilber. You were not only an athlete at the Air Force Academy but you were a very valuable athlete as well as a team leader. You have coached soccer everywhere from the club level all the way up to the college level. You have a wealth of experience as a successful coach in addition to your military and academic leadership. You've demonstrated successful leadership behaviors at the corporate level. Is there one person who stands above the other leaders throughout your life to influence you to become who you are?

Mike: That's a great question. You know I have been really blessed with so many great leaders. So many people who have paid attention to and invested in me when I was a kid, when I was in college and early in my work career. It's really hard to single out that one person who has had the most influence.

I think of all the leaders I have had. My soccer coaches growing up. I had great managers in corporate life. I think of the people in the Air Force. It's really tough. When I was living in Las Vegas after one of our Air Force moves, my dad was at Nellis Air Force Base. That was where soccer really took off for me. Growing up in Las Vegas and playing in the soccer leagues there, I was blessed to have two absolutely world-class professional soccer player coaches who really took an interest in me. Coach Vince Hart from England and Coach Oscar Ferreyra from Argentina. The care they showed toward me and the time they spent with me put me on this path. They introduced to me to a way to play the game that I had never seen before. To play at that level with that kind of passion became my example.

When I was young, I trained under Oscar. He was my club coach. Here was a guy who was so good. He played so beautifully and it just really ignited the passion in me. I think a lot of people have coaches like that. You know, those who are an example of what good looks like.

Oscar went the extra mile. At the same time, he really saw something in me that made me really want to respond. He worked with me a lot and taught me many things. As we were moving to another location, as Air Force people do, and I was going to spend my last couple months with him, he was almost panicking. "I have so much to teach you. So many things that I want you to learn before you leave." He said, "Just promise me you'll give back to the game all I've tried to give to you." The impression he made on me stayed with me for the rest of my life.

Richard: That's really very interesting! One of the things I like to do when I speak to people about leadership is to ask them that question about who had the greatest impact on them. Just about everybody will think "Hmmm." They'll look back and they'll be able to come up with a name or two. Usually it is someone who took just such an interest in them. Someone who cared for them as more than just one of the players on the team. That memorable leader wanted to teach them more.

I found that those who have been very successful in leadership such as yourself have a little bit more difficulty in identifying one particular person. They have had a handful of leaders, so it is difficult for them to select a single individual from that group. The people who have been successful in leadership have had those additional influences over the years.

Now I'm sure that in addition to Coach Ferreyra, you have had some other effective leaders. Maybe not as inspirational but certainly effective. They got the job done. Maybe they weren't as memorable as Coach Ferreyra. What was the difference between those effective managers who led your team to get the job done and those managers who were able to lead the team to a higher level of performance and really hit that level of inspirational leadership?

Mike: You're absolutely right! I could probably name fifteen or twenty individuals and I think of them often. I almost compartmentalize them based on what they taught me and what they represented to me. Whether it was in the Air Force, in soccer, or in the corporate world. So many different lessons.

I really think it was a combination of their passion and their expertise. They are obviously very good at what they do. That is why I respect their opinion, their coaching, their mentorship. But I think it's really their passion. If they're doing something they love, that really excites me. At the same time, they care enough to share that with me.

When you have that combination of passion, expertise and the attitude that "it's not about me, it's about them" or "it's about my team.", that is very contagious. I don't know how you can be in the presence of people like that and not be so excited that you want to go run through a wall for them.

Richard: Run through a wall and keep on running until you are told to stop?

Mike: Absolutely! You run through the wall and you keep going. A military leader says "Jump" and you say "How high?" Sometimes people laugh at that response to authority. It could be survival, in which you know you have been given an order to save your life. But usually it's because this is a person you respect so much that, when they say "jump" you say "I am going to try to get higher and higher and higher."

You know when you are in the presence of people with passion and expertise and they really care about you. They push you to levels that you would not think that you could achieve on your own.

Richard: In our experience in the military, caring about your people is obvously important. There has been a bit of a different perspective from some folks regarding that issue. I have heard the comment. "You've got to be careful about caring too much for your troops. If you do, you are not going to want to send them out on dangerous missions."

In civilian life, that was phrased differently but the sentiment was similar. It was more like "You know Rick, you have to remember that you hired your people. You didn't adopt them." I'd like you to address that type of attitude and discuss how they may or may not have your affected your experience with leadership, whether it be military, corporate life, or coaching.

Mike: I really think that you can never care too much or have too much concern for your people.

Whether it's the military and you're putting them in a position that they're putting their lives on the line or in a less dangerous position. I was never a combat commander but certainly with the military that I was in, that was the culture. If I had ever been put in that position, I hope that I would have been able to do the right thing.

I will always find it interesting that it's a person who doesn't have military experience who thinks that the military leaders think that way. Military leaders are the last ones that want to put their troops in harm's way. But they're also the person who will have the discipline to accomplish the mission and know that this is what we're called to do. I think when they care the most about their people that doesn't mean that we don't put them in tough spot. That just means that we are darn sure committed that we're going to get them prepared. That we're going to give them the tools and the resources and everything they need to be successful.

That level of concern for your people can never be too much. You think about how we lead people and we manage things. The way we can do that is by inspiring our people. Our people are the reason. The results of our team and our organization is what our people do, not what I do as a leader.

I've got to have my people as motivated, confident and directed as possible. I think it's really hard to do that if they don't think that you really do care about them. People have a job, and they'll do their job. If people have a team, they'll play on that team. But we're asking for championship performance. We're asking for above-and-beyond in the level that differentiates winning teams from losing teams. That performance is not easy. It means that everybody is really rowing at the same time, in the same direction. We care about each other and again I think that's a result of a culture that the leader creates.

I've never seen a winning culture that isn't based upon unbelievable caring about the livelihood and wellness of everybody. I've never been a part of an organization whose members perform at a championship level that really doesn't love each other.

Richard: Mike, we talk about caring about the individual as well as caring about the mission to be accomplished. Mission accomplishment is very important to anyone in a leadership position. You are trying to accomplish a task that you cannot accomplish by yourself so you need to form a team.

As a coach, it may be victories and team development. As a military leader it may be seizing an objective. To a business leader, perhaps it is increasing profits or the selling of a company. Does this mission accomplishment relate to caring about the individuals? What is more important, mission accomplishment or caring for people?

Mike: As a leader, the accomplishment of the mission has to be paramount. That is what we're paid to do. As a leader, I want to win as much as anybody. At the same time, I can't do that at the expense of my people. Otherwise I may get a short-term win and that results in a long-term series of losses. I have to put my people on par with the mission but the mission always comes first.

My focus as we prepare for the season is that we know that we're only going to be as good as all of us are in filling our individual roles. As the leader of the team, as the coach of the team, I have to make sure that I've got them prepared. That they have the resources to do that job. The training to do that job and the understanding to do that job and create a culture where they want to do that together.

All of that is time that you will spend in caring about each one of those people. They're not robots and every person is different. Every position is different. There are different skill levels so I can't just cookie cutter the process.

In the old days we talked about managing people as though they were things, and they're not. You lead people. That means that it's going to be important to understand that every person is different. Think about a gene pool. It's probably 99.9 percent common between every human on earth. That 0.1 difference is all the differences we see every day in each individual. It just shows you just how unbelievably complex and beautiful the human experience is. Understand that, and you know how challenging it is to have a high-performing team.

Richard: Mike, it has been said see that "true leaders don't recruit followers, they develop more leaders." You have many very experienced, talented athletes on your squad from year to year. You'll have an athlete who progresses from a raw talented freshman or sophomore to a player who can develop into the role of a leader on the team and possibly become a captain. What do you do to convince your team captains to adopt the same concern for people?

Mike: We look at leadership development here at the school as a full-time job. Developing leaders on my soccer team is a four-year process. It's important that they know followership is a form of leadership. We try from the very beginning when they come in as freshman to talk about leadership. From the very first day you get here until the day you graduate we want to develop you to be the very best leader you can be, while you're here, as well as when you move on to bigger and better things.

It's amazing, because the subject focus will be different each year, whether we're talking to freshman, sophomores, juniors or seniors. It becomes very real during their junior and senior years. They know they are in charge of the team. "This is your team." When anything happens to anybody on the team, as soon as I find out that they're okay, my second call is going to be to the leader of that person. We have our team divided into families. You know in a minute who the captains are. I'll call them in and say, "Where were you? What do you know about this? Where were you when this was going on?" They've got to realize that everyone on their team is their charge now. It's their team. They've got to take that leadership role. They've got to understand they can't be in hiding. They can't say, "Oh, I was just looking the other way!" They've got to be out there. They've got to be among everybody on the team. They've got to know what's going on so hopefully if someone is doing something that's not very smart for themselves as a team, they're stopping it and saying "Hey, let's get out of here. Let's make a better decision." They are there to make sure that everybody's okay after it's happened.

We very deliberately try to get them to adopt a mentality that the team comes first. If you move into more formal positions of leadership, others will be looking to you as a leader, even if just because of how many years you have been here. You have to understand that your mindset must be different. It's not about you. It's about the team. It's about the welfare of everybody on the team. We use servant leadership; a Christian view of leadership in which first will be last and last will be first. I take care of my troops. I make sure that that I'm trying to serve the people I have. I didn't come to **be** served but **to** serve.

Richard: That's excellent Mike. There is one more point I'd like to discuss before we wrap this up. The title of this book is *"DE**SERVE** to LEAD."* You have mentioned that athletes come along as raw freshman. As they become juniors and seniors, they find themselves in a leadership position. Have you ever run into a situation in which someone has reached that "time in grade" but they haven't developed the skills or the selfawareness to lead? Maybe they're lacking somewhat in their traits and their talents to keep them from deserving to lead?

Mike: Absolutely. In fact, each year in the spring semester, we spend a lot of time with our juniors who are going to become our seniors. We want to make sure they are prepared to take over the team as they become the senior class. A senior class has to have very high standards. Those standards now become the minimum for the team. If you don't feel that you can live up to those standards, you almost have to make a decision to eject. The athlete needs to be honest and say, "I cannot be a senior on this team if I am not willing to set a good example. As a senior, I set the minimum standard for the rest of the team." If you're not a person who can really do that, and you're not the person who tries to get out in front of everything, then that's a discussion that we have to have.

Everybone is going to have skill sets. So get out there if that's your skill set. If that's your strength, get out there and lead. I look at it as deserving to lead. It is not because you have a title. Absolutely not! It's because the situation demands leadership. If you're the only person there or you know the urgency of the need, act. When in charge take command. Your influence is greater than your position.

You may have a sophomore who has great leadership influence on the rest of team and I encourage that behavior. Don't wait until your senior year to lead. Know your influence. That's what I mean by deserving to lead. As a freshman, sophomore or junior, performance is going to determine how much influence they start with as a senior but it's never too late to begin that process.

Richard: Mike, that philosophy shows in the successful records you have reached not only on the field but also in terms of graduating quality people with Belmont Abbey. Just to wrap this up, I have known you for many years. We have spent many hours talking about leadership, the excitement of what you can achieve with it and of the influence you can have on people. I want you to share the significance you have achieved by leading people. It is worth all the frustration and responsibility you will experience to reap those rewards?

Mike: I can tell you I'm a soccer coach because I love the game of soccer. It's a passion for me but that's not what keeps me doing it. That's why I love being at the college level. I think it's one of the last good careers where you can get to enjoy seeing players grow from their freshman year to when they graduate. To see the way they act. The way they carry themselves. The way they care about each other and the way they look out for each other and then to see them when they've gone on to graduate. I have former players who are pretty old because I've been coaching for thirty years now. I was only a couple years older than they when I first started coaching. Than means they are only a couple years younger than me now. I see them and they're very successful. They're raising great families. They're leading great organizations. To me the reward is just to see that. What fills my heart is to see what they're doing.

SELF- LEADERSHIP

"An investment in yourself is the best return out there. When you're betting on yourself just go all in."

"The process is not only to <u>see</u> it, it is to <u>design</u> it, and the most important is to <u>be</u> it. That action phase is critical. Action is really where the wow and the results come into play."

--Tiffanie Trenck

RICHARD BROWN

It could be argued that "Empowering others to step into their life" is a subject that might be better included in a self-help book, rather than a discussion of leading others through service. In my opinion, nothing could be further from the truth. The principles espoused by Tiffanie Trenck in her efforts to encourage and assist women to "See it, design it and be it" travel hand-in-hand with the most fundamental of leadership efforts. The only difference between the two is the size of the audience; many versus one.

Principles of self-leadership belong in a foundational position for any preparation to lead. In order to lead others, you first must have the ability to lead yourself. Tiffanie is a stellar example of that ability. She has grasped the responsibility and authority for her own life, as well as the mission that she has given herself to accomplish with both hands. Tiffanie pursues that objective with a passion that is contagious.

Forsaking a successful corporate career in favor of striking out on her own, creating her own organization and assuming the risk of its success in order to empower women to live the life that they have dreamed is leadership par excell-lance! John Maxwell, our nation's foremost expert on leadership development has said "True leaders do not recruit followers, they develop more leaders." At its core, that is what Tiffanie has committed her life to; helping other women develop their own self-leadership skills.

The passion and commitment Tiffanie displays on a daily basis is awe inspiring even on my own best days. Her efforts to help others lead themselves into a life of significance, however they define it, is clear to anyone who comes in contact with her. Her relentless enthusiasm for what life has to offer anyone willing to make the commitment to chase it, can restore the visions of our own lives that we all had as youngsters when we had the temerity to dream.

RICHARD BROWN

TIFFANIE TRENCK

CEO & DESIGNER OF "MORE LIVING"
LICENSED RESULTS MAP STRATEGIST

As the owner of Tiffanie Trenck LLC, Tiffanie unlocks vision and success strategy. After twenty years in corporate America as a top performing Director of Sales in the golf and fitness industry, she has now transitioned to empowering women and companies to step into the life of WOW instead of one of regret, and to OWN IT. As a designer of MORE LIVING, her approach to personal and professional growth veers from the traditional through a unique modernized chic vision technique. She focuses on positive forward vision, strategic activation mapping and strong accountability. Her boutique-style custom retreats, workshops and private mentorship are high in transformation, connection and bold in direction resulting in gla**MORE**ous **LIVING**.

**SEE IT. DESIGN IT. BE IT.
TIFFANIET.COM**

Richard: Tiffanie, first, I would like you to tell me a little about yourself. Let's go back in time to when you started to lose your baby teeth. When you were seven, what did you want to be when you grew up?

Tiffanie: Oh! I like this time travel question! Seven, as we know, is a magical age. I can have a lot of fun with this question.

At seven, my eyes were just wide open. I did dream big, and I did not hold back. My philosophy was to color outside of the lines. My approach was fierce. I think pure joy would be a great term at the age of seven. I ended up naming my current bike today "Pure Joy."

Richard, I think another word at the age of seven is freedom. Most days I would get home from school, ride my bike and just unwind by rallying the neighborhood troops and going off to explore. To answer your question, I don't think I had a set profession I was tied to at the age of seven. Maybe a rock star, travel agent, designer, party planner, doctor, master sales woman, all rolled into one. Something along that line.

Richard: That is one of the wonderful things about that age. At the age of seven, we don't have restrictions. We don't say "Well, I messed this up, and I can't do this, or, I don't have the grades to go to medical school." You are seven and you have the entire universe ahead of you that can unfold the way you want it to unfold.

I know your family environment was a very positive one. Tell me how that family environment supported or hindered your dreams at that point in time.

Tiffanie: Absolutely! That is something I am very proud of. Some people might say "yawn, yawn." I had a blissful childhood but I've learned to really embrace that, especially in the personal development world. A lot of people share stories of pain in the early years and they are stories that really pushed them to help others in their current capacity, which is fantastic.

My story-line is a little bit different. I had a story of love and that's what really pushes me to serve others today. I applaud my parents, grandparents, friends and everyone who was a part of my life. They helped me fill my childhood with love and opportunity. We did have our moments. I think everybody does. There were cloudy days. It was not a perfect life style, but I had a great support system that really did fuel my dreams and still does to this day.

I am full of gratitude and appreciative to them. They are the why I do what I do on those tough days. All I have to do is think about family and friends and then the inspiration hits pretty hard.

Richard: When I hear of that type of upbringing, the term *"Leave it to Beaver"* type of life style comes to mind. As you may recall, *"Leave it to Beaver"* was a situation comedy from the 1950s and 1960s portraying a classic suburban lifestyle of a young family. June Cleaver was the mother. Making dinner and taking care of the household, she always wore her pearls, and Ward, the dad, was never without a tie whether it was a weekend or not. You saw this idyllic suburban life-style. Even then, there was a character named Eddie Haskell who would enter and wreak havoc.

Tiffanie: Oh, I remember Eddie!

Richard: So, even *"Leave it to Beaver"* had some of those moments of stress. That presents its own degree of challenge. I've heard the analogy before that as you go through moments of stress it's like your guiding hand, whether it be God, the Universe or whatever you reach for as a higher power. The purpose of our maker is to apply that pressure to shape us in ways that will determine our destiny in later years.

But sometimes, when life is idyllic, I think folks who have lived your lifestyle are at a bit of a disadvantage. Not that anyone should pity them, but they may not have had those stresses that tend to shape others who were less fortunate. On a more positive note, the people who have had significant stresses seem to learn many valuable lessons as a result. So, you are at this stage of life now where there is something you want to do. How did that "vase" get formed from "Oh, I'll be a doctor or a travel agent. I want to do a million different things at the age of seven." How did that time shape your life's goal now?

Tiffanie: You know, as I got older, and that dream activator mode, my mind set of abundance verses scarcity and coloring outside of the lines began to fade, I started to mould to what society says is a good life. I started to miss those colors a little bit more. I put the permanent markers away and got out the colored pencils. I started coloring inside the lines. That can be much more comfortable. I subscribed to that for a long time. However, I did get my boldness back and brought out my bright colors again. That was one thing that has really shifted as I matured.

A second part to that, which really stands out to me daily, is the shift of maturity. Out of college I was a fierce go-getter. I was playing the big games. I was successful, working hard. I will admit I didn't really have a clue about money management. My parents were beyond generous in all the right ways and I was grateful for that. I was not the sixteen-year old who was handed over the car with the red bow on it in the drive-way. I was still getting dropped off in front of the high school at sixteen. Seventeen rolled around and I got the hand-me-down car from my dad. I don't think it fully matched what a seventeen-year old had as far as the ideal joy ride but I was very fortunate that I had a car.

Eventually, when I started in corporate America and began to see success and have money of my own, things changed. I'll never forget the day

I marched right into the Mercedes dealership thinking I was all that and negotiated a deal on my dream convertible. I look back at stories like that and some of the superficial material ways that define what society calls the rich life. I was very fortunate in that the red lights eventually went off. I hit pause and really had to redefine my success story and what I saw as a rich life.

When I define that today and rewrite that chapter, it's much different. It is about love and relationships with family and friends and living out my purpose. I am a big experience person. I love to spend money on experiences just living in the now or being present making each moment count. That's what I call rich in today's world.

Richard: Apparently, you have changed a bit from when you graduated from the University of Northern Colorado. You went out into the real world and got your big kid job and your big kid paycheck. After that, a transition took place from the material goals that most of us have at that age. Life became more fulfilling and more rewarding from a stand-point of giving to others. Was there an experience that caused that to take place or was it just maturing?

Tiffanie: You know, that's a great question! After college, I was boldly ready to put my big girl panties on and seriously take on the world. Looking back now, I think my life goal was still being shaped at that point in time. Richard, you and I have had conversations before. You so eloquently speak in your brand about the puzzle pieces of leadership. After college, I think I did somewhat of a respectable job putting the corner pieces of my life's puzzle down. But I just had so much work to do to complete the picture, I think I grabbed for some of the wrong pieces at times that really didn't form the image I was looking for.

I worked in the golf industry in high school. After I graduated college, I walked in to see the general manager of the golf course where I had my high school run. I wore my fancy career clothes and had my positive attitude on. I thought "I am sure he's going to hire me on the spot because I am really smart now that I have a four-year degree." I was sure he would want to pay me millions of dollars. Just get this done. If it was only that easy, right?

He explained to me that he didn't have any salaried positions open. All the positions were hourly. He then offered me the very interesting task of coming up with a job proposal that he wanted to look at the next day. So just like college, I had to cram that night to construct a proposal of what I wanted my life and my job to look like and come back to him the next day. To my surprise, he said yes to the proposal! Of course, that was minus the millions of dollars I had originally expected.

Richard: He left some zeros off the end of the salary figure?

Tiffanie: Yes, there were quite a few zeros that were missing! I simply love that story. It is one of belief and I knew he believed in me. That was leadership shining bright. I was developing but still had a weak skill-set at that point in time. I was a true alpha type, and he opened that door for me to thrive. I was very fortunate to have many other leaders to follow that opened doors of opportunity for me.

Richard: That's a unique story. I can't think of a better way to see what's in a person's mind than to say, "You tell **me** what you want to do. You tell me what your job should look like." It's an excellent technique of pulling something up from inside the individual. I think that sort of approach could be very positive in having the person tell you what their dedication and commitment level is. So, did you sign on with that individual after that little test?

Tiffanie: I did! That was really was my transition from working in the bag room at golf courses in the hourly position to going off to college and coming back and beginning a real career.

Richard: Tiffanie, it sounds to me like you had a wonderful childhood and a very supportive family. You saw the world ahead of you and knew you could be anything you wanted to be. We all face challenges in life whether it happens to us personally or to someone close to us. As you were growing up and living in Colorado in this timeframe, there was a very tragic event that took place. I would like you to relate that to us. How the reality at that point in time impacted the dream of that younger Tiffanie. I am certain you know what am talking about.

Tiffanie: Absolutely! Let's jump to that huge impact moment in my life. It was in 1999. I was in corporate bliss. I was working hard. I was learning by the moment, advancing in my career, getting ready to buy my first house and life was good. As you said, I had a very good upbringing, a childhood that I was proud of and a very loving household with a lot of smiles. And then a phone call came in.

I was at work. I was in the middle of a big transitional meeting. The golf course where I worked at the time was getting ready for a buyout. I was in the meeting trying to figure out if I was going to have a job tomorrow or not. The call that came in was from my brother.

To this day, I get choked up every time this comes out of my mouth. There's a reason for that. I know all of us have that story of impact. This is my story. My brother was calling to say he was safe and had just left Columbine High School.

Talk about completely changing course! I no longer had any worry about my job, if I was going to have one tomorrow or not. My number one priority and all that mattered was the love and safety of my family. That day really shifted me for that day and many days to follow. Columbine was really my awakening.

I was fortunate that my brother and my future sister-in-law were safe. Unfortunately, a lot of families didn't get that same ticket. It caused me to do a lot of work to have love override fear and I take that into my life and business today.

Richard: We've talked about that story and the one thing that strikes me is that you painted this… I wouldn't say an ideal childhood but a peaceful, wonderful childhood. That type of life can change in a heartbeat. In high school, it can change in a class period, it can change in thirty minutes. If you're driving a car it can change in a split-second and we never get warning when that's going to happen.

That's an important lesson for us to take into life. If we are sitting here waiting for the next thing to happen, we have no guarantee we are going to get that opportunity. I appreciate you sharing that. I know that it is emotional for you. I was in that area at the time but wasn't intimately involved as you were. I know the Columbine tragedy is a demanding thing to talk about. Thank you for sharing that with us.

Tiffanie: You are welcome.

Richard: I would like to make a transition at this point. Now you have this first big kid job. As you look back on it, is there anything you would have done differently to prepare for entry into the workforce?

Tiffanie: You know, the one thing I would tell my younger self would be just to breathe and trust the journey. That everything happens for a reason—everything. Trust in the process and trust in the steps.

I would also stress that it is easy to get addicted to being busy. I am excited that I now have a strong system and tools, and that has truly helped me balance my life and work with a rewarding outcome. But I think we can also fall into a reactive mode, so I would also make sure that I would avoid being busy and focus on being productive to achieve a rewarding outcome.

Richard: That's great advice in any type of leadership situation. With respect to self-leadership, trust is one of the big three. The concept of being able to define busy verses productive is important. I think a lot us fall into that trap.

Now we are going to make another transition. I've known you in the golf industry and now you are making a big leap. You are leaving your golf comfort zone, which is okay, because we know that in golf, comfort zones are short-lived. What has motivated you to take that leap from the nest?

Tiffanie: If we are going to talk golf talk, we only get one shot at this beautiful thing called life. I've really enjoyed a fabulous run in corporate America. I have had great leaders I learned a ton from. I am so very, very fortunate for that situation and for all the lessons I've had over the years. But that was a season for me. I realized I could stay comfortable in that season for life. But there was another chapter.

My next chapter is one that I am very proud of. It is one of my dream and my purpose. Leaping into it I have no regrets, even on the day when I am sixteen hours and two pots of coffee in, no shower yet. We all know those days.

I am grateful for the journey. I like how you mention the term the "leap." It's such a fun term to me. You always hear them say, "Jump and the net will appear." I jumped off the high dive. You might say I did a cannonball. There was no net. I revise that statement today to say, "Jump and you are going to have to work hard to sew your own net."

Another saying is to "Jump and grow wings during the free fall." The leap into my own business, GlamMOREous Living, which is about helping ladies live the life of their dreams has been very rewarding as well as a test. Talk about self-development! I don't think I've had more self-development ever before in my life. It has been a true sense of accomplishment. Yes, my movement is still growing. I continue to hit debris in mid-air every day and that's part of it.

Richard: That is another great analogy! When you mentioned free-fall, I've been fortunate to experience jumping out of an airplane (a perfectly good airplane at that) but I can tell you this; the parachute was never deployed before we left the plane. That was something that had to be deployed on the way down. When you jump out of the door, that parachute isn't open and you must have the faith that it will open.

So here you are. You've taken this leap out of your comfort zone. Now you are going after some strong life rewards for your own personal goals and mission. I know you well enough to know that you have tremendous strength and numerous talents. But there are those periods of fatigue, of weakness, of self-doubt that crop up and that inner voice says "Really? What makes you think you're good enough to do this?" Do you ever deal with that sort of thing?

Tiffanie: Richard, no! Are you kidding? Yes, of course. Daily! Self-doubt is a very dangerous disease. We all have these voices. I've just learned what is important is how we manage those voices. I hear them every day.

A kind of a fun thing that I've done to control that voice is that I ended up naming her Tess. Tess only knows the past and fear and she can't see the future. So, when Tess surfaces I just acknowledge her. I know she's there to protect me at times and I thank her for caring, and then, I release those thoughts. That sounds a little foolish, but it really helped to say, "That's a Tess thought!" It's a lot easier to wash this away when we talk about that noise and that self-doubt.

I think others can really play into that as well. You don't need to accept doubt from others. What counts is really believing in yourself. I am a firm believer that whether it's God, the Universe or whatever belief system you have, its gifts really aren't delivered until you personally unwrap them.

Richard: That's a splendid example. The dedication you have and what you want to bring to other folks is very impressive. Tell us something about that. What is your mission with "GlaMOREous Living" and what are you trying to do? What's brewing right now for our readers?

Tiffanie: I want to be very clear. I think the term "glamorous" can be very misunderstood. I spell glamour in my company a little bit differently. "g-l-a-m-o-r-e," and I stress "glaMOREous" living so "more" living. It is about giving ladies the skill set to live the life of their dreams verses just thinking about it. Truly owning the outcome and taking the necessary step to accomplish it.

We're only designing one life. I emphasize that one life in business and personal still equal one. I know we discussed changing lives and I love that you challenged me by asking, "Do you really want to change anyone?" No. People are perfect just how they are. I think a better term in my mission is to impact lives for the better. It's a true comfort zone for me. It's my passion and I am so excited that it has come to life. It has taken a lot of work. I love to meet new people and learn about their visions and lives and assist them any way I can to make it a reality. So, come say hello to me! I'd love to meet you. A good first step is to visit my website. It is:

www.TIFFANIET.com

Just come say hi and we can start some fun conversations!

Richard: I think it's wonderful what you're doing. The women in your generation as well as mine were sometimes limited in life based on the assumptions of others. When a woman would say, they want to be an astronaut back in my day they would hear

"Oh honey, you can't do that!" There were so many restrictions placed on women. Society has kind of thrown that off in most cases but it's hard to get it out of our head. That's one of the biggest strengths about what you do: helping to make women believe they can do anything. It's not about glamour. It's all about "MORE."

I just want to know if you can offer any closing words of advice to any of our audience members who are considering making their own giant leap to happiness and significant success, however they define that?

Tiffanie: Absolutely! I think this is my favourite question!

First off, you know I would say to the audience that an investment in yourself is the best return out there. When you're betting on yourself, go all in. Talk about a great present to yourself !

Start by finding your vision. I state this in my company daily. The process is not only to **see it**, it's to **design it** and the most important is to **be it**. That action phase is critical. Action is really where the wow and the results come into play. That is number one; invest in you.

Number two is to surround yourself with a solid tribe and a mentor you know. You can't go on this journey alone so be careful. Handpick who you want. I'm very proud to say you are part of my tribe! Thank you for that and for just being you and all the support and guidance you have provided me. Tribe members and mentors are a big component.

Number three; live in the now, just be present. When that flight comes in that takes us to our destination home, I don't think that airline gives us a pre-boarding call.

Richard: Not so much.

Tiffanie: No, I don't think we get the pre-boarding call on that one. The message there is just to live life full-out, be present, live in the now, live a legacy. It doesn't matter if you have $5 or $5 billion to your name. It's living a life that you are proud of. It's never too late to make a change and reroute in a new direction.

I am kind of a big analogy person so let's stick with the plane theme as we go to number four. That's when you run into obstacles. In business and life, I will just encourage you to ride it out. Don't change planes, or pilots. Turbulence is normal. Stay on course and I can't stress this enough; be open to failure because it is life's best lesson. Success really does follow a lot of bruises, bumps and broken bones. As much as we all love microwaves, there are no microwaves in preparing your legacy. You must do the work. I mean you really must put in the time and energy to see the results.

Number five; this is a very important key component. Just say yes. Say yes to opportunity, and say yes to life.

www.TIFFANIET.com

THE LEADERSHIP SPOTLIGHT

"Leadership is the ultimate means to an end. Leadership is completely selfless. If you are not thinking about those you lead, the goals that they have to accomplish, or what you've asked them to commit to, you are providing an environment in which you are going to get a team that's not pulling together. "

"Commitment is such a huge part of being a leader. If you use the word "try" you are setting yourself up for failure."

—Len Dubois

RICHARD BROWN

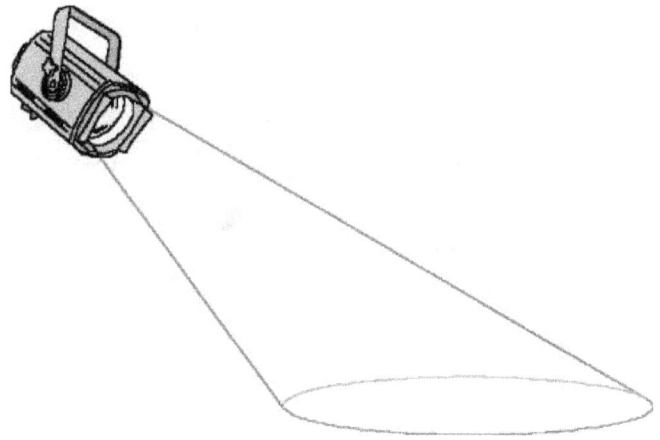

There are few opportunities fraught with more potential for disaster than making a good first impression in a foreign environment. Everybody is looking at the "new guy" or "new girl." When that transition occurs to a former military officer, still with a regulation haircut, surfacing in a corporate environment for the first time, the stress can be palpable.

A young, immature individual will stand to lose significantly in that situation. The tendency is to seize the moment and take a dominant, assertive position at first appearance. Not a good move.

I could observe my next interviewee in exactly that situation because I was the man who hired him. As he stood squarely in the spotlight during his first meeting with his new team, his maturity and emotional intelligence shone brightly. Len Dubois knew enough about the industry he was joining to begin his journey, but more importantly, Len was fully aware of what he didn't know. That can be more important in that situation that what you do know.

Through the rest of our time together, I saw what made Len Dubois an outstanding Army officer, and more importantly, what has made him a very successful leader. Len gets it. From his awareness of the need for commitment to be demonstrated in his own actions as well as expected from those he leads, to the trust that he must generate from his charges, to the importance to knowing his people beyond simply their employment history, Len consistently shines brightly in the heat of The Leadership Spotlight.

LEN DUBOIS

**VICE PRESIDENT OF MARKETING
TRILLIUM SOFTWARE**

Len Dubois directs Trillium Software's Global Marketing team and is responsible for the strategic direction, development and execution of worldwide marketing initiatives. Len has been a senior executive in the high tech industry for more than 20 years and has deep experience and expertise in selling and marketing complex software solutions across multiple vertical industries. He created the award-winning Trillium Software System® brand for the company's flagship software, recognized as one of the top enterprise solutions in the data quality industry. He has spoken at data quality conferences in both the United States and United Kingdom and has authored many articles on data quality and Customer Relationship Management.

Len is a graduate of University of Rhode Island and Harvard Extension School.

Richard: Before we get started, I think it's important for our readers to understand why I requested this interview with you on this topic and I think it's important for you to understand that as well. As one reads your bio from the standpoint of the military, from the standpoint of business and from the standpoint of your family, I believe a certain truth emerges about you. In the formal leadership positions you have held, you've demonstrated your ability to lead people and to lead organizations, otherwise you wouldn't be in the position that you are.

The one thing I wanted to say is that I had the great honor to work with you for about five years. I was a district manager, and we had twelve people that that were salespeople. One of the things you always demonstrated was a tremendous amount of self-leadership. You were an individual who didn't need to be motivated. I don't believe one person can motivate other people. I believe you can provide an environment for motivation, allowing people to motivate themselves. That is always what I saw from you. Self-motivation and a drive to succeed. The other thing that came through was your peer leadership within our team.

You provided a tremendous amount of peer leadership to that group and that is never an easy task. Okay, enough of my efforts to give you a big head. Lets get to work.

My goal here is to simplify leadership. One of the points I would like to make to people is that as a leader, you tend to go through the day, performing your daily tasks without fanfare or recognition. It is often difficult to identify who the leader is at first glance. It's in other more significant moments that come up every once in a while that put the leader in the spotlight. They make you realize "Well apparently I've got to make a decision!" It is those points that will determine the leader's destiny. Would you share your perspective on this issue?

Len: Just as much as you're in a leadership role, you are looking to provide your team with the things that they need to be successful. What I have found is that people are absolutely looking to you to provide them with the direction and just as importantly, the vision as well as the means to get their job done. If they really like what they're doing—and I always ask folks if they love what they're doing—and they have the means to do what they need, then, it makes their job a whole lot less like a job. It makes it something that they can look forward to coming to every single day. As a person who's in a position of managing not just the company, but a lot of differnt people, I try hard to say, "If I've given them an objective and I have given them the means to do what they need to do, I can step back a little bit as a leader and make sure that it gets done the way I want to be done."

Richard: I couldn't agree with you more. That's exactly the philosophy I have. When people step into that first leadership position it can be a real challenge. New teachers, new coaches can all fall victim to a mistaken philosophy. They want to do one of two things. Either they step in and want you to know they own the world. "I'm the big leader and I know how to accomplish everything we need to get done." Or they hesitate, afraid to lead. The point I'm making is that most of the good people you have, in fact I would go as far to say **all** the good people you have, desire leadership. They don't want to be in an organization that fails. They want to be in an organization that succeeds and they're looking for you as a leader to provide that leadership to them. They are certainly not looking for micromanagement but effective as well as inspirational leadership.

I'd like to know about the very first significant leadership experience you had. We all have it. It frequently falls upon us right around the age of nineteen or so it seems. I am curious what your experience was the first time you went "Oh my, I have some responsibility here!"

Len: That's a wake up moment for a lot of people. My first leadership position was when I was a second lieutenant in the United States Army. I was facing my platoon for the first time. I had forty-four men staring back at me, expecting me to lead them in everything that we needed to do.

The United States Army, or any military, is different than the corporate world. Many of the people who I was facing on that day knew more about how to get my job done in certain instances than I did. In the military, you are really put into a on-the-job training environment. Your job is to determine what it is that these folks need to get their job done. You may not be able to tell them **anything** about how to get their job done. To me that was the most important thing to learn about leadership in the military sense.

I try to boil it down into not trying to do too much as a junior leader. As you said earlier, you want to do everything perfectly. You want to take the reins but at some point it's more important to understand what your role is in the leadership of young men and women.

Richard: General Schwarzkopf talks about Rule 13; "When placed in command take charge. " I talk about that a lot but I think it's very easy to take that the wrong way. To say "OK, I'm the boss now!" You will eventually learn how to get the job done with the people you have. Even in corporate life you would have to admit that you have people working for you now who are more technically proficient than you.

Len: That is really true. I think that as you grow in your career you're going to find that the more important part of leadership is leading people with diverse skills and counting on them, relying on them to be smarter than you or even more skilled than you are in a very specific task. I have always felt if I can get those folks to perform at their highest level and do it as a team, it makes all of our jobs so much easier. It also makes it so much easier to commit to success. Commitment is such a huge part of being a leader. If you use the word "try" you are setting yourself up for failure.

Richard: As you stepped in front of that platoon for the first time, I am certain they didn't just pull you off the street, slap a couple of gold bars on your collar and throw you in front of forty-four hardcore engineers. Do you feel like your leadership training up to that point at the University of Rhode Island prepared you for that moment so that you could come out, stand in front of them and not fall on your sword?

Len: You know, one of the things about my R.O.T.C. experience was that I was so excited about following my heroes into the service and I so wanted to be a good officer that I raced through the first two years. I was able to complete all of my requirements in that time which allowed me to actually go to my officer basic in my sophomore year and not my junior year. The ability to do that also gave me high rating amongst my peers and it allowed me to have a fairly significant leadership role back in the R.O.T.C. battalion.

I had the opportunity to see many different roles and responsibilities at the platoon level. I was well prepared. The first time I had to call my unit to attention, I was certain they would respond appropariately. However, you never can be completely prepared for every mission. I think one of the traits of a really good leader is understanding that you're going to be learning over and over again as you move forward.

Richard: No question about it. I know that the Army makes fun of the Marine Corps and vice versa, but one of the things those services do really well is not only training you to do the things you need to do from the standpoint of weapons, equipment and that sort of thing, but to teach leadership.

It has been said that leaders don't recruit followers. True leaders develop leaders. To take someone that is a brand new 22-year old, "butter bar" lieutenant and say "Now we're going to pick you up and we're going to put you down in

Germany or in Hawaii or someplace and you're going to lead these forty-four men" is quite a stretch unless there was some previous training along the way. You've been developed as a leader but you know it's not just R.O.T.C. It's something that every leader has a responsibility for in every industry whether they be a coach, a teacher or parent. I know with your kids, you're just not showing them the ropes but you're also developing leadership skills in them as well.

Len: Rick, that is absolutely true. It also goes to the points about caring and trust. I can't imagine how a leader succeeds today without caring about the people who are working for you. Right now I've got a team of about eighteen people. Four or five of them work directly for me. Over my career I can point to four or five people who have been promoted to chief marketing officer or senior vice president in other companies. As a leader it is important for you to focus on the skills and the things that your charges need to do in order to grow them in their career.

The first part of that is to care enough to know if that's what they want. If that is what they want, it is your job as a leader to provide them with those skills and opportunities to succeed so that they can move on. That's what was done for me and as a leader I owe that back to them.

Richard: No question about it. Many supervisors, particularly early in their careers, before they've been successful as leaders understand that they need to care enough to be committed to the mission. "This is why my boss hired me and this is what we're going to get done." We've seen that in our common experience. These leaders are simply concerned with getting the mission accomplished. With that mindset, it is easy for these "youngsters" to lose track of what's going on in the people's lives with with whom they are completing the mission.

Your charges may spend eight to ten hours a day with you but they have twenty-four hours in their day. For fourteen or so other hours daily, events are occurring in their lives. If you're not aware of that and you think that is not going to affect the way they work, you are sadly mistaken. I couldn't agree with you more about he importance of both trust and caring

One of the issues in any leadership position is the reality that you are not always out there in in front of the group. Frequently as you are just going through your normal, uneventful day. Every once in a while there seems to be experiences that will crop up that will shine, in effect, that "Leadership Spotlight" upon you. Now everybody's looking at **you**. If you are inexperienced, your upper lip may begin to the sweat. You are beginning to comprehend "I'm going to have to make a decision here. I wasn't expecting this but now it's on my shoulders and everyone is looking at me!" I like to refer to that as "The Leadership Spotlight."

I'm curious if you've ever had an experience like that as hockey goalie or an Army officer or even in business. In the Marine Corps we called that situation, "What now, Lieutenant?" It is when you find yourself at a decision making point that has the potential to determine your destiny.

Len: I can think of a couple of them that have happened throughout my career. The first one was when I was a junior marketer at Trillium Software. I was in the process of hiring a new manager for the organization. As I was going through the interview process, my boss came to me and said, "Listen, there's a president of another division who would like to see one of their employees moved over to give them a chance at the job that you have open." I said I would be happy to interview the person first, and if they fit, I'd be happy to hire them."

I brought the person on board. About a month after that, my boss came to me and said, "Look I was trying to do the right thing for the company. I was trying to be a good corporate citizen, but I don't know that this person is going to work out here. What I'd like you to do is to give her goals that she cannot achieve. Are you okay with that?"

That was that moment where you say "Wow!" I just looked at my boss and I said, "No, I'm not all right with that." I had only been with the company a year at the time. He looked at me and he said, "Well I guess I'm going to have to do your job for you."

The point I am making is that as a leader, you owe it to the people who work for you to treat them with respect. And if you know this person isn't qualified to do the job, it's my job, **not** my boss's job, to either train them to help them become qualified, or provide them with the opportunity to move on. To put a challenge in front of them that they couldn't possibly accomplish is the sign of a leader who was trying to do something to make themselves look good, as opposed to trying to do something to accomplish a real goal.

Richard: That must have been a difficult time for you. It would have been very easy to just say, "Well, that's what the boss wants me to do" and just go ahead and do it. That would have been the easy decision. With that course of action, you wouldn't have gotten heat from your supervisor but you would have known it was the wrong thing to do inside. I refer to that as a "Hard Right versus the Easy Wrong" decision. We were faced with those as leaders more often than we should be.

That particular story has been a very common one. "Okay, here's what I want you to do." The leader knows it's going to be easy and agree to do it, but also knows it's the wrong thing to do. Based on their own core values, they must consider taking the hard path and say "Sorry, I'm not going to do that." I salute you for doing exactly that.

The other thing you mentioned was this leader who had a mistaken concept of the Leadership Spotlight. They said in effect, "If I can make the light shine on me, I'm going to be the hero!" I compare that to the arsonist who starts a fire and then shows up and puts the fire out so they can be seen as the hero. Sometimes in leadership you'll see experiences like that where an individual with a little bit of perception will say, "You know, I have an opportunity coming up here to really shine if I manipulate events perfectly. I can make myself be the hero." When the room lights are turned off so the spotlight is on such a manipulative leader, bad stuff frequently takes place. That's a great example! Someone who is willing to manipulate the situation so that they look good, frequently turns out looking bad in that type of situation. Is that something with which you would agree?

Len: I would wholeheartedly agree with that. Even in my early adulthood there's just so many examples of people who talk a good game. A lot of times what happens is that they over-promise, and they over-promise on the backs of people who truly don't understand what their talents are. I truly believe that if you're expecting someone to bring a gift to the table that they don't possess, that's your problem as a manager, not their problem. When I played hockey, I knew I wasn't qualified to be a defenseman or an offensive line player. I was a goalie. I stopped the puck and my coach understood that. Stopping the puck was what I brought to the table.

My hockey coach was a great mentor to me. I'm still in touch with him because I believe he had my best interests at heart. He taught me so many valuable lessons in life.

Richard: I'm doing some work right now with an organization of coaches. They look at themselves as coaches, but sometimes I think they fail to see themselves as leaders. That is unfortunate because their role as a leader is so valuable and potentially so rewarding. It is much more important than teaching the skills of a hockey player or any type of athlete.

You mentioned the concepts of trust and commitment. I'd like to get some guidance from you for those young leaders who are now in that leadership position. They are going to be faced with these decision points, the spotlight moments. Would you share with me some of your thoughts on how you can anticipate something coming up that is going to require you to act in the right way?

Len: The best way to handle those unexpected situations that come up is to do something that Bill Belichick, head coach of the New England Patriots, does better than anybody else that I've seen. He forces his players to think situational football. He prepares his team not just for the play that's in front of them but to think about the options that **may** occur.

While my role today isn't as immediate as a football player's role, it is very important to know what your employees are facing. For instance, our company could be acquired tomorrow. If that's the case, is my team prepared both personally and professionally to take on that new role or to take on that new challenge?

We live in a rapidly changing world. Acquisitions happen. Mergers happen. Employees leave to find other opportunities or follow a dream that they may have and that requires everybody else to have to switch what they're doing a little bit in order for the team to succeed. What we try to do is to practice different scenarios. It's important for me as a leader to say "If I'm going to be short this person or if I'm not going to have this person's capabilities, what's my succession plan? What's my option for the future?" Beyond just being technically proficient, you've got to be prepared to face different scenarios all the time.

Richard: One of those spotlight moments that stands high and above almost everything else in the leadership of an organization is that periodic performance review. You can do a lot of damage in a performance review if you are a leader who has the wrong core values going in. If you're going to behave in a way that's untrustworthy or uncaring or uncommitted, it can destroy your destiny. You can also establish yourself as an inspirational leader by operating with the core values of trust, caring and commitment. If the sun is going to come up tomorrow, there could be moments that take place today that will determine your destiny as a leader. Your behavior is going to determine your success. It's not behavior that reacts to the situation but it's behavior that is simply integral to your core being and the way you lead.

Len: I want to add one more point to what you just said because I think it is crucial to this issue. One of the things that's really important to me is quarterly sit-downs with my team to make sure that I understand where they are. I give you one example. I've got a director who right now who is dying to be a vice-president. I keep looking for an opportunity for him to practice the skills of the vice president of marketing for this organization so that he can then take that and move forward in his career. I wouldn't know that unless I sat down with the person, made an effort to know him and found that out. I want my leaders to sit down with their folks and say, "What is it that you want out of this job? What is it that you want out of life?" If their personal development isn't important to you, then their professional development doesn't matter.

Richard: Caring, and caring about them as individuals and people, not just as employees or names on an employee roster. I would like to give you an opportunity to wrap this up with some sort of slam-bang finish coming from all the experience you've had and all the thought that I know you give to leadership. In conclusion, can you give our readers one more thing relating to your philosophy of leadership that could help them tomorrow in dealing with their people?

Len: I think leadership is the ultimate means to an end. Leadership is completely selfless. If you are not thinking about those you lead or the goals they must accomplish, or what you've asked them to commit to, you are not providing an environment in which your team will be able to effectively pull together to work towards a common goal. My feeling as a leader is that I have to provide a vision for all of them to be self-succeeding. Honestly, I don't know how you can do that without caring about who they are as young leaders.

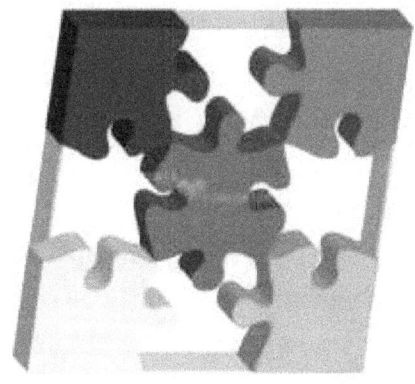

CONCLUSION

Five individuals. None of them carry the type of fame that would cause the general public to recognize them. In fact, they wouldn't recognize each other if you put them in the same room. Open a bar in that room and I can guarantee you an enjoyable and entertaining happy hour. Close the bar, introduce an objective to be accomplished and I can assure you, leadership will flourish.

How can I be so sure? Because I have seen each and every one of these individuals demonstrate trust, caring and commitment as a fully integrated core value. Take their words from their separate interviews to heart.

Now for the bonus. My purpose for interiewing them was to record for you accounts of what I have personally witnessed. These are dedicated individuals who have demonstrated commitment, trust and caring for others in everything I have seen them achieve. My intention was to have them expound on those seperate core values, one at a time, to give the reader a personal perspective with which to relate.

But a funny thing happened on the way to the publisher. During each interview I noticed a interesting interaction take place. Colonel Dotterrer's discussion of commitment began to shift into a discussion on the importance of commitment to taking care of your troops. The same occurred with Connie Schroeder Grosse. Her discussion on mission statements again shifted to the importance of servant leadership. Meg VanderLaan's excellent points on generating trust concluded with her testimony that deflected credit for her achievements from herself to her team.

Without a microscope, you can see the same interactions taking place in all of the interviews.

My analogy describing leadership as an image similar to a puzzle provides an answer to why this took place. After you have located the vital corner pieces, placed them on their appropriate spots, you begin to join edge and center pieces. If your image contains a small spotted dog, you don't look for a piece with the dog on it because experience has taught you that rarely will a single piece contain the entire dog. You look for a tail, or an ear with a spot. The remainder of the little fellow will be found on a seperate, but interlocking piece.

The tactics that provide relevance to effective and inspirational leadership interlock as well. Rarely will you find the answer to a leadership challenge completely contained in one tactic or core value. They all interlock. Every piece, every leadership maxim such as "Leaders eat last" can be traced eventually back to one or more of the corner pieces that you initially placed, namely, commitment, trust and caring. Violate the principle by jumping to the head of the chowline, and you will experience the heat and pressure of the Leadership Spotlight.

RICHARD BROWN

Does this paint an intimidating picture for you? Good. It should. As my friend Connie Schroeder Grosse explained so elequently, and I am certain that my other friends will agree, "The rewards of leadership of that sort will far outweigh anything that you will be required to exercise to become an effective and inspirational leader."

So dump out the box. Start at the beginning. Lets find your four corner pieces together and begin your journey. In that way you will demonstrate the fact that you do indeed:

DE**SERVE** to LEAD!

About the Author

Richard Brown

Richard has been putting together his own leadership puzzle for his entire adult life. That includes his college years, which are rarely included in anyone's definition of a d u l t .

As a midshipman enrolled in the Naval R.O.T.C. program at Oregon State University, he was one of two selected to serve in a midshipman officer position as a junior. In his senior year, he served as Midshipman Battalion Commander, the highest leadership position available to a student. Named the USMC Honor Graduate, he served his active duty as an infantry officer with the 1st Marine Brigade in Kaneohe, Hawaii. Prior to leaving the Corps, Richard was selected ahead of his peers for promotion to captain.

In 1978, he began a 33-year career in sales with Pfizer Inc. Four years later he was one of the youngest individuals at the time promoted to District Manager. In 2001, Richard returned to the field to apply his experience to the most challenging type of leadership, leading his peers.

Richard helped found PRE, or Professional Resource Enhancement, in 1998 as a means of bringing his unique vision of leadership to small businesses, coaches, teachers and young adults. After retiring from Pfizer in 2012, Richard has dedicated his "second adulthood" to exploring, discussing and teaching **leadership** to those who desire to accept that challenge.